15 Seconds of
BRAVE

ALSO BY MELISSA DOYLE

The Working Mother's Survival Guide
Alphabet Soup

MELISSA DOYLE

15 Seconds of BRAVE

The wisdom of survivors

VIKING
an imprint of
PENGUIN BOOKS

VIKING

UK | USA | Canada | Ireland | Australia
India | New Zealand | South Africa | China

Viking is part of the Penguin Random House group of companies whose
addresses can be found at global.penguinrandomhouse.com

Penguin
Random House
Australia

First published by Viking in 2022

Cover illustration by Sybille Sterk/Arcangel
Cover design by Christa Moffitt, Christabella Designs
Author photograph by Nick Leary
Typeset in 13/19 pt Adobe Garamond Pro by Midland Typesetters, Australia

Printed and bound in Australia by Griffin Press, an accredited
ISO AS/NZS 14001 Environmental Management Systems printer

A catalogue record for this
book is available from the
National Library of Australia

ISBN 978 1 76104 486 1

penguin.com.au

MIX
Paper from
responsible sources
FSC® C009448

We at Penguin Random House Australia acknowledge that Aboriginal and
Torres Strait Islander peoples are the Traditional Custodians and the first
storytellers of the lands on which we live and work. We honour Aboriginal and
Torres Strait Islander peoples' continuous connection to Country, waters, skies
and communities. We celebrate Aboriginal and Torres Strait Islander stories,
traditions and living cultures; and we pay our respects to Elders past and present.

To the incredible people in this book who trusted me to tell their stories, and to everyone who needs a little help finding their own strength right now

Contents

Foreword

I initially considered writing a book about resilience for personal reasons. At the beginning of 2020 my fiftieth birthday lurked ominously around the corner. Meanwhile *Sunday Night,* the public affairs program I hosted for Channel 7, had just been cancelled and I'd begun to worry my future with 7 – the station that had been like a home to me for twenty-five years – might also be in doubt. On top of that my firstborn child was not only getting ready to leave the nest, he was getting ready to leave the country! As these cracks began to appear in my world

I became anxious, melancholy and unsettled and, for the first time in my life, I had trouble sleeping.

Having spent decades reporting from the front line of news in Australia and around the world, I knew my worries could easily be filed under 'first-world problems'. I also knew, however, that millions of other women faced personal crises of one kind or another as they careened headlong into the often confounding crossroads of middle age. I thought a book about ways to cope with personal upheaval might be of help.

Then the coronavirus pandemic hit and everything changed. Suddenly all of humanity – men, women and children alike – was feeling deeply uneasy and uncertain. Infection and death rates quickly soared; millions lost their jobs when businesses closed and entire countries were locked down. Economies sputtered, people were separated from loved ones and friends, and the nation's mental health took a corresponding dive.

And yet . . . life went on. Sure enough I *did* lose my job at Channel 7, I *did* turn fifty and my son *did* eventually move to America to study. Against the depressing backdrop of a one-in-one-hundred-year global crisis these developments didn't seem so bad after all.

Like everybody else, I tuned in to the news each day during 2020 with a sense of dread. I'd digest the statistics, absorb the health messaging and wonder how on earth society was going to come through the other side of the COVID crisis. I listened as people in government, the medical field and the mental health space explained that we were in uncharted waters, that there was no guidebook or policy blueprint when it came to a worldwide killer virus. While that was largely true, it occurred to me there *were* people we could turn to for wisdom in times like these. They were all around us. I'd even met plenty of them.

Over a quarter of a century in the news business, I've been privileged to interview thousands of people from all walks of life, including many who have survived calamity, suffered unspeakable trauma or lost everything they owned. Some were victims of crime or circumstance, others had their lives upended by twists of fate. However, one thing they almost always shared – and which constantly amazed me – was the strength and endurance of the human spirit. Some of these people have had a lasting impact on me and changed my outlook on life. You'll hear from them in the following pages.

In the years since I started work on this book, the world has felt more out of control than when I began. At the time of writing, the pandemic had killed 6.2 million people, and only now is it finally showing signs of tailing off. The dark cloud of war has descended over Eastern Europe with

Russia's invasion of Ukraine, while closer to home deadly record floods in Queensland and New South Wales have been a reminder that climate change poses a serious threat to our way of life.

As natural as it is to feel apprehensive about the future, engaging again with these remarkable women and men has buoyed me during the most turbulent time I can remember. As difficult as their journeys have been, I'm grateful for their candour, their courage and their wisdom. I have learned a lot from them. I hope you will, too.

One

Tonya

The first time I encountered Tonya Whitwell, in 2017, just over a year had passed since her quiet, happy life in the Brisbane suburbs ended, and a traumatic new existence appeared in front of her. It's no exaggeration to say she was the most broken person I'd met in all my years covering the news. Emotionally, Tonya was on her knees. It showed in her tired eyes, and she told me with a fragile half-smile that she was hardly sleeping at night. Knowing in broad brushstrokes what Tonya had endured, I dared not ask about the thoughts that stalked her in those cursed hours of lonely wakefulness. That would have been cruel.

I felt a strong connection to Tonya straight away. Both mothers of two and both adoring of our fathers, our emotional ties overlapped in a way that made me feel very deeply for her. As we spoke, though, I quickly became acquainted with Tonya's quiet strength, her natural grace and her dignity – characteristics she'd clearly carried over from her old life into the new; traits she would need more than ever as she confronted a future no one could ever imagine they'd have to face.

I've often reflected on Tonya's painful odyssey when facing upheavals of my own. Her mantra, borrowed from J. K. Rowling – 'Rock bottom has become the solid foundation on which I rebuild my life' – is a rallying cry for anyone who has been laid low by personal tragedy. In Tonya Whitwell – whom I have been privileged to get to know better over recent years – we have a beacon of hope: living proof that no matter how far we may fall into despair, there is always a way back to the light.

Around ten o'clock on a Monday night in 2016, Tonya heard a knock at the door of her Brisbane home, followed by the sound of muffled voices in the living room. She'd gone to bed early but her husband, Garry, had answered the door and let the two police officers inside. When Tonya came out from the bedroom and saw the uniforms, she assumed they were there about the recent burglary of her house. Instead, the solemn-faced officers turned to Tonya and said her father, Robert Whitwell, had been found dead in his home in South Australia.

The blood drained from Tonya's face as disbelief, grief, shock and confusion rolled over her all at once. 'How?' she gasped at the police as Garry put his arms around her. '*When?*'

The apologetic officers were short on details and gave Tonya the number of the detective in Adelaide who was handling the matter. With trembling hands, Tonya phoned the officer in South Australia only to be given patchy information. Her father's body, the detective explained, had been discovered by a neighbour who'd grown concerned when Robert's newspaper was left untouched on his front lawn. The cause of death was still unknown.

The awful absence of detail only worsened Tonya's heartache and her imagination raced to fill the void. Perhaps her dad had had a heart attack, or a stroke. What if he'd fallen? Whatever had ended the life of the hale and hearty eighty-one-year-old, Tonya dreaded the thought her darling dad had died alone. He'd lived with his second wife,

Joyce – Tonya's stepmum – but she'd developed dementia and was in a nursing home. Robert visited her every day. Now Joyce would never see him again.

Tonya had always been extremely close to her father. 'I was a real daddy's girl,' she says as we chat about her childhood in suburban Adelaide. Robert was a kind and gentle man. He had integrity and respect for others, and he was a little old-fashioned in his ways. His impeccable manners matched his immaculate appearance, and he always kept a comb in his back pocket.

Robert's devotion to his family never dimmed. When his first wife, Avis, left when Tonya was twelve, he knuckled down to raise Tonya and her brother, Justin, on his own. 'Dad went through a lot of heartache,' Tonya says as she mentally leafs through memories from the '80s. Back then single fathers were a rare breed indeed. 'Mum just went off and did her own thing and moved to Queensland, but Dad was the stable one. We had the same family home for twenty years!'

And now, in what felt like a heartbeat, he was gone forever. By eleven o'clock on that Monday night, the terrible enormity of it started to sink in. With a broken heart Tonya let her children – twenty-four-year-old Ryan and nineteen-year-old Brittney – know what had happened. They were the worst phone calls she'd ever had to make.

Brittney was driving home from a trip away and answered from her car. 'I told her the police had just come and her Poppa had passed away,' Tonya recounts softly. 'Brittney burst into tears – *hysterically* burst into tears.'

The following morning Tonya held her children close when they met at Ryan's house and prepared to catch a flight to Adelaide together. Brittney seemed particularly knocked around by the sudden family tragedy. She'd driven through the night to make it home on time and looked exhausted and dishevelled. She chain-smoked, too, something she never normally did in front of her mum.

In Adelaide the shaken trio checked in to a motel not far from Robert's house where, over the following days, the extended family gathered to grieve. Tonya tried to comfort her distraught kids as much as they tried to protect and comfort her. She'll never forget the image of Brittney sobbing on the shoulder of her Uncle Geoffrey, Robert's brother.

After five days in Adelaide there was still no news on the cause of Robert's death. Tonya was adamant she'd stay in South Australia until the coroner released his body and gave some clarity and the opportunity for some answers. Meanwhile, Brittney and Ryan flew home to Queensland: Ryan had to work, while Brittney needed to deal with the apparent theft of her car.

Tonya took a room at the home of her cousin Judy in Wallaroo – a quaint little port town a couple of hours north-west of Adelaide – and waited. Finally, twenty-one days after Robert's body had been discovered, Tonya's phone rang late in the evening. It wasn't the coroner's office, but a detective from South Australia's Major Crime Investigation Branch. He said he needed to see her urgently – in Adelaide. Tonya pointed out how late it was, that she was 160 kilometres away from the city, and asked why they couldn't talk over the phone. Oddly, the detective insisted they had to speak face-to-face.

In the end a compromise was reached: two local officers were dispatched from Wallaroo station to sit in the lounge room with Tonya and Judy while the detective phoned again from Adelaide. 'I didn't know what was going on!' Tonya recalls. 'My mind was running a hundred miles an hour. We finally got the phone call – the two policemen were sitting there, not knowing anything, they were just there for us – and the detective on the phone told me how sorry he was that he had to tell me my daughter had been arrested for murder.'

For Robert's murder.

In that split second, with a phone pressed to her ear, Tonya's old life shuddered to a halt and a darkness engulfed her. In this horrifying new reality her gentle, smiling, mild-mannered dad was a homicide victim, and her only daughter was his accused killer. The detective continued, telling her that Brittney's girlfriend, Bernadette Burns, had also been charged over the murder. Tonya clutched desperately at the hope there had been some kind of mistake. 'I thought, "Surely Brittney didn't do it! It must have been Bernadette!" My mind started going into this whirlwind of emotions and I really don't know what else he said to me.'

As news of the arrests started to break on radio and TV bulletins, Tonya phoned her husband, Garry, Ryan and her mother, Avis, in Brisbane. Tonya needed them to hear it from her first. It was the first tug on a thread that eventually unravelled Brittney's dark and secretive life for all to see.

Like millions of kids around the country, Brittney had grown up in the great outdoors, under the huge Australian sky and the protective wings of her loving parents. The family enjoyed camping and fishing, and often Poppa Robert would fly up to Queensland from Adelaide to join in their adventures.

Robert loved being a grandad. He'd fly in for birthdays and other special occasions, too, and when he couldn't he stayed in touch by sending letters and photographs in the mail. Brittney would write to him as well, and in the school holidays she was always excited to join Tonya for week-long visits to Adelaide.

Brittney had been an active and energetic young girl. She played sport, and rode her bike and skateboarded in the quiet streets and parks near their home in Beenleigh. She climbed trees and fences, was adventurous and happy. When big brother Ryan left home at eighteen, thirteen-year-old Brittney had her mum and dad's complete attention.

After she started at Trinity College, however, a worrying change came over her. Brittney's first year was particularly challenging, and Tonya and Garry were alarmed when she was accused of bullying other students. They dealt with it swiftly, engaging a counsellor to address what appeared to be an issue with anger. The following year, though, the shoe was on the other foot when Brittney became the victim of bullying. The skateboarding and tree-climbing stopped; she retreated to her bedroom and shut her parents out of her inner life. When she started to self-harm by cutting herself, her worried parents sought professional help again.

By seventeen Brittney was back under the care of a psychologist. Tonya, who urged her to stay in school and complete Year Twelve, describes her daughter at that time as a 'moody teen' who was strangely attracted to dark imagery. A fan of Lady Gaga during the 'Little Monsters' era, Brittney grew obsessed with knives, blood and late-night visits to the cemetery.

When she finished school at eighteen, Brittney wasted little time in removing herself from the gaze of her parents' watchful eyes. She left home to live with friends but struggled to get work beyond a part-time job at a pizza parlour. Tonya says it was during this aimless period that Brittney started going right off the rails – something Tonya was only made fully aware of in the aftermath of Brittney's arrest. At the time Tonya and Garry had no idea their daughter was leading a very troubling double life. When the colossal reality check came in the wake of the murder charge, it was as bad as any parent's worst imagining.

'Drugs,' Tonya says with a rueful shake of her head. 'She'd started when she was about fourteen. And not just marijuana – heroin and cocaine and all the hard stuff.'

Tonya and Garry weren't naïve when it came to teenagers, but Brittney's mastery of deceit and duplicity had left them completely in the dark. When police spelled out the ugly truth for them, they were as gobsmacked as they were devastated. 'We thought she'd been going to school,' Tonya says, 'but she was off prostituting herself during the day instead.'

Prostitution, the pocket money Brittney had received for doing chores and her meagre earnings from the pizza shop apparently weren't enough to bankroll her spiralling addictions. But she knew someone who had plenty of money. All she had to do was go and take it.

Like a surprisingly large number of people from his generation, Robert Whitwell didn't trust banks. The retired public servant had worked hard all his life and at eighty-one still had $115,000 in life savings. His suspicion of corporations saw him slowly cash out his shares and stash money around the house instead. The hitch in this homespun approach to money management lay in the fact that Joyce's dementia gave rise to a few unsettling habits. Fearful she might accidentally burn the house down – and all of their money with it – Robert decided it would be safer padlocked in his garden shed.

Tonya clearly remembers the day in April 2016 when he phoned to tell her about this new arrangement. 'I said, "Oh my god, Dad! What if some drug dealer found out?" And he said, "Who's gonna know?"'

Brittney had been standing right next to her at the time.

Then nineteen, and evidently desperate for cash, Brittney formed a fairly unsophisticated criminal plan. With a friend in tow, she packed her silver Holden Astra and headed south on a gruelling 2000-plus-kilometre trip from Brisbane to the northern Adelaide suburb of Craigmore, where her Poppa lived.

Robert's neat red brick house was in a quiet cul-de-sac full of other neat red brick houses. It was the kind of safe, cheery neighbourhood where kids on bikes ruled the street and people knew all of their neighbours by name. Of course everyone knew the affable Robert and Joyce.

A silver-haired gent from a bygone era, Robert was always friendly and took as much pride in his tidy garden as he did in his personal appearance. He was spritely for his age and proud of his family.

Brittney and her friend rolled to a stop across the road from his house, far enough away to be inconspicuous but close enough that they could case out a burglary. They had booked in to a nearby motel, and after watching Robert for a few days, the young women discovered he was a man of routine, leaving home at the same time every day to spend time with his beloved Joyce, who had recently gone into a nursing home just a short drive away.

Brittney's friend at one point messaged her: 'He's lovely! He just said hi to me,' and Brittney responded: 'Don't get too attached he may have to die.'

Desperate to ransack her Poppa's shed for the fabled treasure, and too impatient to wait until he had left, Brittney and her friend broke in late one night while Robert was asleep. Brittney used a milk crate to jump the fence and opened the garage roller door for the other girl. Woefully amateurish burglars, they crossed the backyard to the shed but a neighbour came out and spooked them before they could figure out how to overcome the simple padlock. They fled unseen, though the next morning Robert noticed the milk crate suspiciously propped against his fence and the roller door ajar. He called the police, then rang Tonya.

'It was ironic because the time that Dad told me that story, our house in Brisbane had been broken into,' Tonya remembers. Robert also mentioned he'd seen a car with interstate plates in his street. The last person either of them would ever have suspected to be behind the wheel was Brittney.

One hundred and fifteen thousand is a figure that would scratch at the mind of any addict and, a few months later, Brittney was keen to try to rob her grandad again. It was August 2016, and this time she took a new accomplice, her girlfriend, Bernadette Burns. The young lovers drove for twenty-two hours to Adelaide, arriving on a chilly Friday morning and parking across the road from Robert's house. Brittney wasn't waiting for her Poppa to visit Joyce. Leaving Bernadette to put on her make-up in the car, she crossed the road and knocked on his front door.

Robert was surprised and delighted to see his granddaughter. He'd had no idea she was coming to visit. Nor did he know she had a knife hidden under her clothes. Hurrying her in from the cold, he put the kettle on.

As winter sun streamed through the curtains, they nursed cups of tea at the kitchen table and leafed through photo albums brimming with Kodak memories of family holidays gone by.

Warmed by the nostalgia, Brittney had second thoughts about the evil she'd crossed three states to unleash. When she texted her misgivings to Bernadette, however, her accomplice messaged back: 'Just harden up and do it.'

When they'd finished their cups of tea and their stroll down memory lane, Robert walked Brittney to the door. As he bade her farewell, Brittney pulled out the knife and stabbed him in the neck. Then she knifed him in the chest before once more stabbing his neck. God only knows what went through the poor man's mind.

Robert staggered back into the kitchen and collapsed onto his chair. As unfathomable as it sounds, Brittney fetched a bandaid and helped him apply it to the gruesome wound in his neck. She handed him a cloth for the hole she'd made in his chest, too. And then she washed their teacups at the sink as Robert slumped at the table – still strewn with their cherished memories – and bled to death. Brittney watched as his life drained out. When his last breath was spent, she texted Bernadette to say it was done.

The two began a frenzied search of the garden shed and the house but couldn't find Robert's money. They snatched

$1000 from his wallet and a few pieces of Joyce's jewellery before setting off for the long haul to Brisbane . . . posting happy selfies on Facebook along the way.

Police later found $98,000 in the garden shed and $30,000 secreted inside the house, as well as the girls' 'kit bag' in the car – knives, masks, duct tape and cable ties.

'He was my dad and my daughter killed him.'

Talking with Tonya as she recounts her story, this is the sentence I find almost too difficult to absorb. The grief that comes with a homicide is complex. It's a horrifying way to lose someone – at the deliberate hands of another human being. However, I've covered enough murder trials to know the victim's family isn't the only party that suffers. Cold-blooded killers have loved ones, too – innocent mums and dads whose lives are shattered by their own grim visits from the police. Their grief should never be diminished.

Often the anguish of parents whose offspring have killed is weighted with shame, and even guilt. The question 'How could I have raised someone who'd do such a thing?' inevitably arises. Tonya Whitwell is the only person I know who has straddled these awful roles: victim's daughter and mother of the accused. A very lonely place to be.

It was an anonymous call to Crime Stoppers that led to Brittney and Bernadette's arrest; a friend had heard about the murder, and knew they'd made an unusual trip to Adelaide. Phone records marked their journey on a map and, faced with all the evidence, Tonya was forced to come to terms with Brittney's latticework of secrets and lies. It goes without saying it was not easy for her to do. 'I thought I'd raised her right and I trusted her,' Tonya says quietly. 'But the police show you the evidence and you finally come to realise that, yes, they were right and, yes, she did do it.'

Investigators laid out a sobering dossier of Brittney's life as an interstate drug runner and small-time crook. 'She was on ice and had hooked up with drug dealers,' Tonya reveals. 'She was doing all these drug runs . . . the police had found out her car had been in Sydney and Adelaide, and we lived in Brisbane!'

As she plied the nation's highways in her silver Holden, Brittney would carry 20 litres of petrol in a jerry can – taken from her father, Garry – so she didn't have to stop at service stations. And instead of staying in cheap motels, she'd roll out a tent or sleeping bag at impromptu campsites by the side of the road, the logic being that petrol stations and motels have surveillance cameras that might have recorded her illicit activities and left pixelated breadcrumbs should the drug squad have taken an interest in her.

Tonya pauses, appearing to mull over this level of cunning and criminality. 'It was weird things like that, that we found out afterwards,' she says, scrunching her nose at the unlikeliness of her child honing such underhanded tactics. 'You know something's not right at the time, but you don't know the whole story.'

It turned out the burglary of their family home was another betrayal. When Tonya and Garry enjoyed a short weekend away camping, Brittney tipped off some associates that the coast was clear and they could ransack the house. 'They stole iPads and anything worth money,' says Tonya. 'Brittney knew that we were going away that weekend. The dog was in a pet motel, so not home to guard the property. She let them know that no one was in the house and said, "You can go in."'

On remand in Adelaide Women's Prison as she awaited trial, Brittney put Tonya on the 'Do not contact' list and outright refused to speak to her. 'Right from the beginning I knew where I stood,' Tonya says. 'I knew why. I had so many questions to ask – and she did every deceitful thing that you could possibly think of – so she didn't want to face me.'

This is the first time in our discussions that Tonya's anger trumps her sorrow. 'She would speak to Garry and Ryan,' she says pointedly. 'Garry drove down there at the beginning and went into the jail, but Brittney just had that blasé attitude that it's somebody else's fault and it was never her fault.'

Tonya and Garry struggled to communicate as they dealt with the crisis in different ways. 'I didn't know how to make it right for him and he didn't know how to make it right for me,' she says. 'We were two people going through the same traumatic situation, but I wanted to know everything and he didn't want to know anything.'

Their eighteen-year marriage crumbled. Within the space of six months Tonya had lost her dad, her daughter and her husband in the most terrible circumstances imaginable. She was also at risk of losing herself.

I can't imagine grappling with what Tonya had to face, let alone navigating such a tempest without going under. 'How did you manage to keep going?' I ask her.

Tonya says her long journey towards solace began with acceptance – a ground zero of sorts that was extremely hard to reach at the outset. 'There was so much that we didn't know,' she says. 'But by the time we'd seen the proof the police had, you *have* to accept it because you're sort of stuck, you're back-pedalling, you don't want to believe it. It's your daughter, you don't want to believe that.'

Nearly two months later, Brittney confessed. Major Crime Detective Brevet Sergeant Damian Britton says it was when police confronted her with all the evidence that she finally opened up. 'It's shocking that somebody so young could be so callous,' he says. 'She wanted to watch someone die.'

The murder weapon was never found. Brittney said she threw it out the car window on her trip back home.

On top of acceptance, some healing came about through the application of justice. Brittney's sentencing fifteen months later was a line in the sand that Tonya stepped over to begin to move ahead with her life. 'I've always said there are consequences for your actions, that's how my kids grew up,' she says evenly. 'She's got to pay for what she did.'

Brittney pleaded guilty in the South Australian Supreme Court and was sentenced to life imprisonment, with a non-parole period of twenty-one years. Bernadette Burns was also handed a life term with a non-parole period of thirteen-and-a-half years. Tonya was there to see justice dispensed. Brittney was twenty years old at the time but, as she sat in the imposing wooden dock, Tonya says she looked more like a twelve-year-old girl. 'She just glanced over at us to see who was there,' Tonya remembers. 'It didn't really seem like she cared too much.'

Brittney showed no emotion either when Robert's brother, Geoffrey, read his victim impact statement to the court. 'I believe you are truly a dangerous and evil person, and deserve the highest penalty that the law permits,' he said.

Justice Kevin Nicholson was also scathing. In reference to the family discovering it was Brittney who had committed the crime, he remarked, 'It is not possible to adequately summarise the distress and profound anguish.' Tonya felt the weight of his words more than anyone else, and she endorsed him sentencing her only daughter to life in jail. If Brittney is ever granted parole, she'll be forty-one by the time she tastes freedom again. Tonya will be seventy.

The sentencing marked the end of a fifteen-month-long ordeal. Tonya had struggled every day to catch her breath amid the nonstop media attention, public speculation, misinformation, court hearings, lawyers, coroners and floods of tears. It also ended the necessary but draining communication with police – a constant reminder of the hellscape she'd found herself in. Each phone call from well-intentioned detectives stirred up feelings Tonya was desperate to lay to rest. When it was all over, she thanked them. 'We hugged, and that was the end of it,' she says. 'It was a *big* part of my recovery.'

Still, years of pain, anger and sadness followed. Emotional trauma can affect the body physically as well as psychologically, with symptoms ranging from shock and extreme grief to headaches, lethargy, even nausea – all of which Tonya experienced. Her grief was complex. Losing a loved one to homicide is not only intensely traumatic, it is comparatively rare. Robert Whitwell's death was one of 231 homicides in Australia in 2016–17, a relative drop in the ocean considering 184,504 Australians died from all causes in the same period.

A death in the family like the one Tonya experienced is sometimes called 'ambiguous loss', when there's no opportunity to say goodbye and no potential for the kind of closure that helps us heal. The family of someone with dementia may experience this, or people who have a loved one disappear.

To a degree many of us experienced ambiguous loss as COVID reordered our lives. We mourned the freedoms, spontaneity and sense of safety we used to have. We lost jobs, businesses, lifestyles and plans. Some aspects of our lives were irrevocably changed in ways that are as yet impossible to define.

Instead of aiming for closure after loss, psychologists will often advocate for building strength and acceptance. Tonya took all the steps mental health professionals advise. She asked for and accepted help, her doctor prescribed antidepressant medication and she started seeing a counsellor. In addition to talking (and crying), Tonya received some valuable and simple advice from her counsellor: 'Shower every day, wash your hair and remember to do the basic things.'

This self-care regimen became invaluable. 'I used to have massages because that's an hour that I wasn't thinking about other stuff, plus they make you feel good,' she says with a smile.

She also focused on the fundamentals of existing, which similarly allowed her to step out of her emotional skin for a time. Deep breathing, for example, became an important part of her day. 'By the time you do ten deep breaths you're in a different frame of mind,' Tonya explains. She also devoted time to yoga, regular exercise and just breathing in the fresh air. 'Sunshine is a big thing for me, too,' she says.

The beach near her new home on the Gold Coast became her little slice of heaven. 'I used to just walk up and down, up and down, feeling the sand on my feet. I didn't want to be curled up in bed.' It was a slow process, she says, but over time and by putting one foot in front of the other 'you do start to see things differently'.

Of course, Tonya's entire life looked different to what it once was. 'I was no longer a wife,' she says. 'I felt like I'd failed as a mother. Then I thought, "Who am I? I've been a mother and a wife for so long, so . . . who is Tonya?"'

To look for the answer she took her mind back to happier times – her teenage years in Adelaide with her brother and their doting dad. Maybe that formative period held clues about the woman she became but who was now lost to her? Tonya used one of her great loves – music – to unlock emotional doors in her journey of self-discovery. 'I've always loved the eighties,' she says with a girlish roll of her eyes. Using Spotify, she'd cue up playlists bursting with tracks that were ingrained in her heart. Jon Stevens' album *Starlight* was a favourite and she put 'Devil in My Heart' on constant repeat.

'As a teenager I had all this ambition: what I was going to do, who I was going to be,' Tonya says. 'And I was so close to my dad back then, too.' The bittersweet playlists stirred long-lost memories of people, places and the dreams she once had. 'I'd listen to the songs and remember, "Oh yeah! *That* was the nightclub I used to go to. *That* was the boyfriend I had. *That* was the car I drove." Everything just started coming back. So, bit by bit, I did find myself again.'

For a woman who has carried such sadness, Tonya's smile comes more easily today. And she's willing to let it shine on others. A by-product of her profound loss is the compassion and empathy she now has for others in pain. Becoming so intimate with her own vulnerability has shown her that everyone has a story, that all of us struggle at different times.

'I'd quite often sit on a bench at the beach and someone would sit next to me and I'd think, "You don't know how broken I am,"' Tonya muses. 'You can sit right next to someone and not know anything about them.' As she reconnected with herself, Tonya decided to try to connect with others, too. 'I'd *talk* to the people on the bench,' she says. 'I've met people who had cancer and they're all doing the same thing as me, just trying to find a good place and a happy place to get their mental health right.'

She tells me about a little book her cousin bought her, called *The Grateful Heart*. 'It's about always finding good in every day. You can find something even when you're going through this turmoil. When your life is out of control, there are still some people who are worse off than you.'

Her favourite quote is 'Be gentle with yourself, you're doing the best you can.'

If acceptance, and justice for her dad, were the pillars of Tonya's healing, I want to know what part forgiveness has played, and if it is even possible for Tonya to forgive Brittney for what she did. 'If you'd have asked me that two years ago I would have said no,' Tonya replies. 'But time does change you. I don't know if "forgive" is the right word, though.' She cannot put her finger on a word that would do her complex feelings justice just yet.

Tonya acknowledges that some of her family will never find it in their hearts to forgive Brittney. 'But they're also not going through what I am,' she points out. 'She is *my* daughter and it was *my* dad. It's not like some stranger did it and I can just hate them, or not know anything about them. I know everything about her!' Tonya catches herself. 'Well, in saying that, I didn't really, did I? But she is still my daughter and that does make it hard.'

After initially blocking her mother, Brittney has attempted to make contact, only to discover the sands of time have shifted the balance, and Tonya now finds it too hard to face her. 'She's written to me a few times and that's really sad, and takes me a while to process,' Tonya says. 'It always is my plan to reach out to Brittney one day, but not yet. I've tried and I just turn into a blubbering mess, so I know it's not right.'

As she gradually reclaimed her life, Tonya learned to be fiercely protective of herself. When, in the middle of Brittney's trial, her employer pressured her to return to her job, Tonya stood up for herself in a way she would never have done before. 'I was getting bullied!' she says, marvelling at the temerity of her boss. 'I said, "Well fuck you! I won't put up with that." So I quit.'

Tonya's refusal to let anyone hurt her again gave her the confidence and the incentive to start her own business — one that evolved naturally from her healing process. At the height of her trauma she started cleaning. 'It was just one room, or one area,' she explains, 'and after I'd done it, I felt so good.'

Even Tonya's senses – which had been dulled by trauma – helped to lift her back up. 'It was the smell of the products!' she says brightly. 'It might be eucalyptus or orange scent, but it was another sense that I found! Now I've got my own little cleaning business, and that is what makes me happy at the moment – even if it is cleaning someone else's house.'

The newfound autonomy and sense of purpose was essential to Tonya reassembling her shattered self-esteem and her delightful '80s-tinged persona. She knows her life will never be the same but she's getting on with it, stronger and braver than she has ever been.

For thousands of years body art has been an important part of social, spiritual and personal expression, whether it be clay, natural pigments or piercings. It's one of the many ways we signpost the roads and byways life has taken us down. In Tonya's case, tattoos have become her coat of armour and a way of externalising her metamorphosis over the past five years. 'My pain is all on the inside,' she points out. 'There are no scars – it's just hurting, and no one can see it.'

So Tonya decided to mark each milestone of her journey. Her first tattoo was the word 'Dad' next to a blue rose on the inside of her right wrist. On her right forearm a clock represents the passage of time during her darkest days. She wears the face of an owl with piercing orange eyes on the inside of her arm. 'I'm wiser now, and stable,' she explains when my eyes are drawn to it.

'And the dreamcatcher?' I say, nodding at the design on her upper arm.

'Catching my dreams, of course!' she says, smiling widely at my obvious question. 'Living my life the way Dad would be proud of.'

We talk some more about her father, the old-fashioned gentleman Robert Whitwell, and when I ask how she remembers him, Tonya chuckles softly. 'With his hand on my knee,' she says, and her voice cracks a little with emotion. 'I think that's where my strength comes from. You can't help but cry, but each day is a new day and I look for little signs that he is around me. I can feel him. He wouldn't want me to live my life any other way than to be happy.'

From everything she's told me about him I have no doubt Robert would have been proud to know Tonya is the type of person who strikes up gentle conversations with other injured souls on park benches. Lately those healing encounters have given her the strength and desire to actively seek out Australians who fall victim to unimaginable tragedy. 'If I see on the news someone going through something devastating, something in the realm of what happened to me, I will reach out to those people,' she says. 'I message them just to let them know there is good in the world. I tell them, "You can come out the other side," and I wish them the best.'

Two

Grace

As I was working on this book in October 2021 Australia lost one of its greatest living treasures, Eddie Jaku, at the age of 101. In the Nazi death camps of Buchenwald and Auschwitz, where his parents were murdered in the gas chambers, Eddie witnessed one of the most atrocious episodes in history. In the 1950s, after surviving the Holocaust, he began a new life in Australia. He raised a family, worked hard and volunteered at the Sydney Jewish Museum, where he shared with visitors precious insights from his remarkable life right up until COVID closed the museum in 2020.

Far from being brought low by Hitler's wickedness, Eddie used his experiences under the heel of oppression to point to higher things: human kindness, generosity, love and friendship. Expounding upon these became his life's greatest work. In 2020, at the ripe old age of one hundred, the dedicated peace campaigner penned his memoir, the delightfully titled *The Happiest Man on Earth*.

I dearly wish I'd had the opportunity to meet Eddie Jaku; I'd have liked to hug him and thank him for his book, which is one of the most important I've ever read. Eddie's wisdom is endless but if I had to pick one aphorism it would be this:

'Every breath is a gift. Life is beautiful if you let it be. Happiness is in your hands.'

Over the years I've been fortunate to meet many people who were targeted by odious regimes and lived to tell their stories. Most recently I interviewed Dr Kylie Moore-Gilbert, the Australian academic jailed for more than two years for espionage in Iran in 2018. At her nadir Kylie spent seven months confined alone in a tiny, windowless cell with a television blasting the same Farsi soap opera at full volume all day, every day.

Subjected to emotional torture and forcibly drugged, Kylie told me in March 2021, after her release in a prisoner swap deal, that she found strength and salvation deep within herself. When dragged before a court and sentenced to ten years (on charges she has always denied), Kylie was ordered to write a response to the judge.

'You can do whatever you like to me but freedom is an attitude,' she wrote. 'Freedom is a state of mind and I am free. No matter what you do to me, I am still free.'

It took Eddie Jaku one hundred years to mentally process his life and commit its many lessons to paper, and Kylie Moore-Gilbert is uniquely placed – as an academic and lecturer in Islamic Studies at Melbourne University – to explore nuance and meaning in the ordeal she endured. As I reflected on their stories I couldn't stop thinking of another survivor who'd left a lasting impression on me, someone who'd been comparatively unequipped to process her ordeal. Unlike Eddie and Kylie, she was just a child when a regime tried to steal her from the world.

I first heard about Grace Arach many years ago through my ambassadorship with the humanitarian aid organisation World Vision, and was determined the day would come when I could tell her story. When I finally called her to ask if she would entrust me with it, I could only marvel at her optimism and her easy laugh.

Although we both live in Sydney, we were forced to get to know one another over Zoom (thanks, COVID). It didn't really matter though; Grace's personality is so potent, vibrant and sincere that it felt like she was sitting across the kitchen table from me as her lovely face smiled out of my laptop.

Grace's body language spoke louder than that of anyone I'd ever met. As we talked her arms drew huge gestures in the air and her face lifted skywards whenever she laughed, or gasped at the intrusion of a terrible memory. Grace has an empathy that only comes from a true understanding of pain and injustice – striking for someone so young. I was in awe of Grace from the start.

As usual, her arms were like soaring birds and her head tilted in all directions as she walked me through one of the most harrowing stories of survival I have ever heard.

We started with the day she got shot.

Grace told me she had no choice but to run into a hurricane of bullets in 1997. Her rebel brigade was under attack from government forces in bushland somewhere in northern Uganda. It was her duty to carry the rifle of her commander, Otti Lagony, so Grace was on his heels when he ran towards the crackle of gunfire that day. As a helicopter gunship thudded overhead a bullet slammed into Grace's chest, spinning her in a gruesome battlefield pirouette. Fuelled with adrenaline, she staunched her wounded left breast with a cloth and staggered back towards the rebel camp. If she fought on while bleeding, superstition had it, more rebel casualties would pile up. More guilt. More shame. More terror. As if her life could have got any worse.

Grace should have been at school that day. Instead she was in an army of brainwashed children, stolen from their families and forced to commit atrocities at the whim of a madman.

More bullets rained down from the gunship as Grace dragged herself into a stand of tall grass and mercifully passed out. Later, after the guns had fallen silent, Otti Lagony and his men carried her unconscious back to their makeshift camp, where Grace came to and her waking nightmare began again. Maimed children lay in the darkness. Some had lost limbs. A mortar had torn one boy's belly wide open. Grace listened to him cry until he died.

She insisted her own injury wasn't bad, but it was. There was no exit wound on her back, which meant the bullet was lodged in her chest. For a so-called army, the rebels' jungle-floor triage was pathetic: no medicine, no painkillers, no instruments – just boiling water. A woman poured some onto Grace's wound, causing her skin to slough away like wet paper.

It was just another night in a horrendous ordeal that had begun more than a year earlier. But as she lay in the dark with the smell of blood in her nostrils, Grace reached inward, like she had done many times before, and clung to a gossamer thread of hope. 'Hope came if you got through a battle alive,' Grace tells me, her body strangely still for a moment. 'I had to believe that maybe one day I would go back home.'

Grace had always wanted to 'be someone'.

She was the youngest child and, remarkably, the only young girl in her village near the city of Gulu in northern Uganda. As a feisty four-year-old she'd follow the older kids to school and eavesdrop on their open-air lessons. Although too young to start, the impatient, inquisitive little girl was enchanted by the magic of education.

Her early years were peaceful and settled, even though her parents separated when she was a baby. Grace's mum, Doreen, was a nurse; her father, Godfrey, was a captain in the Ugandan Army. Doreen didn't want to take her place among Godfrey's many wives and chose to make her own life in the village while he travelled throughout the country. Because Doreen worked, Grace spent most of her time at the knee of her maternal grandmother, where she dreamed of her future.

'I wanted to study and I wanted to *be* someone,' she tells me. Her options, however, were limited to the jobs she could see. First she thought she'd be a nurse like her mum, or a teacher. Then she had her heart set on becoming a nun. 'I had even gone to the convent and liked the way they dress,' Grace recalls. 'I said to myself, "Sister Grace. That sounds good!"'

Her grandmother wouldn't hear of it, though. As her father's firstborn child, Grace was required to marry and have children. But no matter what anyone said, Grace wanted more than that from her life. Much more.

Captain Godfrey Lamony was well respected and kind to Grace, even if she found him a little intimidating with his uniform and bodyguards. Whenever he visited, she'd run and hide – scared he'd take her to live with her paternal grandmother and family in another town.

Not long after Grace started school, Godfrey arrived one day unannounced. Forewarned that five-year-old Grace would run, the headmistress held her tightly by the hand. Godfrey assured Grace he only wanted to take her into Gulu for the day, and promised to buy her shoes, a new dress and lots of sweets. He assured her he'd bring her home afterwards. It was a lie. Two days later they arrived in the mountain town of Moroto near Uganda's border with Kenya, where Godfrey lived in an army compound with his new wife, Margaret, and their children.

In Moroto Grace was given the full Cinderella treatment. Her stepmother was jealous and cruel. 'I would only eat when her kids had eaten, and I had to sleep on the floor,' Grace recalls. 'Sometimes her kids pulled the blanket away.' But she was too scared to complain. When her father was away, which was often, she was beaten, too.

Grace silently endured the degradation for four years. Her salvation only came after a concerned neighbour tipped Godfrey off that something was amiss. One morning, in 1993, he left for work but doubled back to the house. Slipping quietly through the door, he caught Margaret beating Grace.

Margaret was asked to move back to her home city, and Godfrey and Grace relocated to the capital, Kampala, 460 kilometres away. These were happier years. Grace and her father grew close. Importantly she liked his new wife, Joyce, who was kind, even when Godfrey was away on duty.

It was a volatile time in Uganda. The country had gained independence in 1962 after seventy years of British rule. In 1971 the government was overthrown by military dictator General Idi Amin and the war to oust him nine years later left a political vacuum. Throughout the late 1980s and early 1990s, a number of parties sprang up in opposition to the government.

The largest and most feared militant rebel group was the Lord's Resistance Army (LRA) led by Joseph Kony, a high-school dropout who styled himself as a Messianic warlord. Kony's militia tore through central Africa like a knife, killing and mutilating civilians and abducting children to use as sex slaves and soldiers. Bizarrely, Kony claimed he was a spokesman for God who took his cues from the Ten Commandments.

The LRA's strategy was to use terror to make Uganda ungovernable, and everyone feared them. If there was the slightest hint Kony's rebels were approaching, entire villages drained of people as families hid in the bush. Eventually they abandoned their homes after dark as a matter of course. 'During the day you stayed home and cooked and then at night you'd go and hide,' Grace remembers.

Before long the LRA started attacking civilians in their bush hide-outs as well. Typically they'd murder adults and kidnap their traumatised children. 'So then,' says Grace, 'there was no hiding place.'

Although she feared them, little Grace didn't fully understand what they were. In her young mind the rebels appeared as otherworldly creatures, certainly not human. One thing she knew for sure, however, was that they'd stolen her cousin David.

In 1994 Uganda's conflict flared as the neighbouring Sudanese government threw its support behind the rebels. Kony's ill-gotten army grew. In early 1995 the rebels drew close to Kampala. Grace and her father were living in a small village outside the capital so she was sent back to the safety of the city while Godfrey stayed behind to mobilise troops.

That same night, 31 January 1995, Captain Godfrey Lamony was killed in battle. The fatal shot had reportedly been fired by Vincent Otti, the LRA's chief strategist and a distant relative Godfrey had known since childhood. Grief-stricken, Grace was returned to her mother in the village near Gulu.

Grace was now a tall, long-limbed adolescent. She was about to start high school and in spite of her heartbreak she was looking forward to losing herself in her favourite subjects: social studies, history and geography.

In his will, Godfrey had instructed his younger brother Martin to pay Grace's school fees. Doreen was now living in the local nurses' quarters and, as Grace couldn't stay there, it was decided she'd live with her Uncle Martin in the village of Pawel, 7 kilometres away. When the day to move arrived, Grace was given a lift by the local Catholic priest, Reverend Father Santos, and four workers, who were travelling by truck to collect firewood from Pawel.

After they'd driven a few kilometres Grace heard shouting and looked up to see a man aiming a rocket-propelled grenade directly at them.

'They were dressed in full army uniform from head to toe,' Grace recalls. 'I asked the Reverend Father, "Why are the soldiers stopping us with a rocket propeller?"'

'No, those are the rebels,' the holy man replied.

The words sent a chill up Grace's spine. 'Are they human beings?' she asked faintly.

After the LRA soldiers stole their shoes and torched the truck, the terrified travellers were marched into the wilderness at gunpoint. Grace's feet were soon shredded by the sharp grasses and rocks as they trekked all day and night with only short rests for food. Grace refused to eat. When the sun rose on the second day, the LRA released Father Santos and his workmen but said they were keeping Grace.

Fearing what lay ahead for her, Father Santos begged them to let her go. They threatened to kill her if he didn't shut up. Father Santos was powerless to help her.

Although they pillaged everything from food and clothing to vehicles and weapons, the LRA's most prized spoils were the children they fed into the ranks of their army with the same cold indifference a shooter might have loading bullets into a magazine. An estimated 60,000 were abducted and exploited in this fashion over twenty years.

After another two days on foot Grace arrived in an LRA camp covered in mud and blood, and close to collapse. In a small clearing in the jungle the makeshift mini village of tents and tarpaulins was patrolled by children holding outsized machine guns: a ragtag army of baby warriors, some in uniform, others in play clothes. Front and centre, and in complete command, was Otti Lagony, Joseph Kony's notoriously brutal deputy.

The camp was typical of temporary LRA bases scattered around Uganda. The largest division – several thousand strong – was based across the border in what was then Sudan (now South Sudan), where Joseph Kony himself was in charge. Roughly half of the LRA's ranks, in both Uganda and Sudan, was made up of other people's children.

Grace had no sooner slumped under a small cassava tree than the sound of gunfire triggered chaos. The LRA fled into the long grass and disappeared beneath the shrubby green canopy but Grace froze in terror. Two rebels returned and dragged her away with them. Later, Grace would wonder whether she'd missed her chance to escape.

'But where was I going?' she asks me rhetorically now. 'I don't know where I was. I don't know what to do. I don't have any skills! No gun! I don't know how to dodge a bullet! And if I run and hide, who is going to find me?'

She didn't know it then but had she tried to escape it most likely would have been her final act. Standard practice in the LRA was to beat deserters to death, no matter how young. Worse still, other children were forced to watch and take part, then smear themselves with the blood of the victims. In Kony's twisted patriarchy disobedience, including the refusal to help murder another child, meant death.

Initiation was also brutal. When the skirmish ended, Grace was ordered to lie on the ground, where she was repeatedly caned by the other children. The older a child was, the more they were caned. And when the next child was snatched, it would happen again – the new recruits forced to participate while still bleeding from their own beatings. The lesson was simple. 'So when they give you instructions,' says Grace, 'you know what to do.'

With her skin swollen and split it was time to move on again. As Grace limped alongside her abductors she uttered her first words since being kidnapped. 'I asked someone, "When are we reaching home?"' she remembers. 'He replied, "There is no home. Where we stay is home."

'We would walk around, no bedsheets, nothing. Because you're too tired you just get the branches off the tree if it's raining. If you're sleeping you have to get up, just keep on walking day and night, day and night.'

Grace was the youngest of the new girls captured by Otti Lagony's unit. Frightened, barely speaking and still refusing to eat, she was placed in the care of an older girl, also named Grace, who'd been a high-school student in Sudan until her future was also snatched from her.

Later, an adult LRA militant explained to Grace how the group functioned. His name was Vincent Otti. After he'd laid down the law, Otti looked Grace in the eye and bragged that he'd killed her father. Grace revealed none of the rage and grief that surged through her veins. She knew it was wiser to stay silent.

The LRA's view of children was as simple as it was sickening: the younger they were, the easier they were to brainwash. Boys were given a gun and a rank, and trained to kill. Girls were distributed among the men as slaves and sexual playthings. As commander, Otti Lagony had first choice; the other girls were handed out to his hierarchy. Lagony chose Grace as his eleventh wife. She was around twelve. He was thirty-five.

That night, the older Grace took her to Lagony's tent. 'Grace said, "You shower, put this Vaseline or something, and wear this dress and these undies,"' Grace recalls with a disgusted shake of her head. 'She took me to the tent and after she left I ran.'

Lagony let her go but two weeks later, when she was again delivered to his tent, he raped her at gunpoint.

Lagony had four child brides and seven adult wives. It was the children's job to prepare his food. Grace was tasked with carrying his hot flask of tea at all times. Whenever they stopped she had to have a fresh brew ready. If he asked for his tea and there was none, Lagony would beat her. She also had to carry his clothes and water.

Whenever they stopped for the night, the girls set up tents for the commanders. Grace was taught to handle a weapon. She was given a short machine gun and told to think of it as her mother and father – the only thing that would protect her. Like the others, she was taught how to disassemble and clean it, and how to shoot to kill.

On top of lugging Lagony's cooking plates, utensils and the all-important tea, Grace also had to carry his weapon, as well as her own, with three magazines of ammunition strapped to her body. Such was the life of a child soldier and sex slave in the Lord's Resistance Army.

The reluctant adolescent soldiers traversed hundreds of kilometres on foot to wage war against government troops. Along the way they'd stop to raid villages, murder civilians and abduct more children to feed the killing machine of Joseph Kony's delusional guerrilla war.

Around a year after she was abducted, Grace was once again weighed down with Lagony's quaint array of battle-field necessities when gunfire erupted and the government bullet tore into her chest.

In agony after she was shot, Grace was still ordered to carry Lagony's gun and kitchen around in the scorching sun. Twice the unit's medic – a man who'd been kidnapped for his skills – tried and failed to remove the bullet by digging into Grace's chest with a knife.

By then her skin was peeling away and a new layer would be torn off every time she removed her shirt. The pain eventually became unbearable, so, several months later, the medic made another attempt to remove the bullet. 'He had medical equipment by that time,' says Grace. 'I felt like he was pulling and pulling and we got the bullet. They don't have anything to stitch with so they leave the wound open and just wash with hot water.'

The suffering was more than any child should be forced to bear, but Grace figured if she could survive being shot, raped, beaten and terrorised, perhaps her spirit could stay strong enough to somehow make it back home. 'Maybe one day,' she would think to herself, 'I will escape.'

No matter how great the temptation, however, running away was an enormous gamble. For a start Grace rarely had a clue where she was, but the main barrier to freedom was the razor-wire fence of fear that had been constructed in her mind. Too many times she'd been made to watch as deserters were rounded up and clubbed to death as an example to other traumatised kids homesick for their parents.

By January 1997, Lagony's group had walked all the way to southern Sudan, where Kony was based. It was the first time since the day she was kidnapped that Grace could properly rest. As Lagony's unit merged with Kony's, Grace joined others in building grass huts and working the land. The days were long and draining as she toiled to help grow enough food to feed nearly 2000 mouths. But it also brought a degree of stability.

Lagony had also been injured in battle and, unable to walk long distances, he was forced to stay in Sudan with Grace by his side. She paints a picture of relative domesticity during this time: an African home setting with kids running around and cows being slaughtered for Christmas. Not that Grace was content, or remotely okay with what was happening to her; rather, she was resigned to her fate and knew the only way to survive was to accept it. At least for now.

'You just realise that this is your reality,' says Grace. 'All you think about is to survive and follow the rules not to be killed.'

The results of brainwashing and the long-term effects of captivity were evident all around her. 'When I was abducted there was a lady, Margaret, who was a lieutenant,' Grace recalls. 'I can see she's happy. So I watch other people, and they're happy. There's nothing else you can do! And you might be depressed or think about home but, with time, you will have to forget.'

In the absence of kindness or a voice of reason, Grace's thoughts sometimes warped reality. 'I was upset,' she says. 'I thought, "My family didn't look for me. Probably they don't really care because no one came for me. Maybe this is the right place I'm supposed to be and then I've got to adapt to it."'

Her guiding ambition, however, was simple. 'You have to survive,' Grace says with a flourish of her lean, elegant arms. 'If you're not dead the following day you hope for the best, that one day you'll get home.'

To that end Grace fought hard against despair because it didn't equate with survival. 'You need energy and if you're depressed, you might not have energy to walk and you'll be killed,' she explains. 'No one babysits you. If you can't walk they'll kill you. That's the rule.'

Grace's captive life played out under the constant gaze of Otti Lagony. He grew to trust her and eventually promoted her into his elite special forces division – a 'privilege' that brought her a degree of security. Lagony had been shot in the face and scarring caused one of his eyes to appear as if it was looking sideways. A menacing visage. Although everyone in the LRA was terrified of him, Grace says she saw a warmer side to Lagony. 'When you see his appearance, he looks like he's gonna kill everybody,' she admits. 'But if you get to know him he's a nice person – that's what

I thought at the time.' Grace now recognises these emotions as the result of total reliance. 'I had become dependent on him. When the right person to love isn't there, you accept the love you are given.'

In a classic case of projection, Joseph Kony demonised the Ugandan Army, which, he said, was out to kill – not liberate – the children he'd abducted. Kony said that if a child *did* somehow manage to escape, their family would no longer want them anyway. Although he extracted a degree of loyalty through rituals and group killings, like any cult leader he infused his philosophy with twisted religious dogma and superstition. He told his child soldiers that a cross daubed on their chests in oil would protect them from bullets.

It's impossible to know whether Kony and his associates figured these techniques out by themselves or whether they studied the psychology of brainwashing. American psychiatrist Robert Jay Lifton, who examined former prisoners of war in the 1950s, identified a number of steps in the brainwashing process. It begins with an assault on a person's identity, breaking down their sense of self. When they are pushed to breaking point, they are offered the possibility of salvation, where small acts of kindness seem huge and the victim believes the captor has saved their life. The final step is the rebuild – an introduction of a new belief system. The victim is made to choose between the old and new, making them feel their fate is in their own hands.

Clearly Grace had been affected by the LRA's mind games, but her inner fire still burned bright in spite of them. She would openly challenge Lagony and even argued with him, which seemed to gain his grudging respect. Grace recounts a moment she interpreted as an act of kindness, such as it was in the evil world view of the LRA. An escapee had been recaptured and brought back to camp to face the consequences. Grace had been earmarked to help murder the child, but Lagony stepped in. 'The first time when they came to pick me to go and kill another person, he said, "No, you can't take her,"' Grace recounts. 'I think, for me, that was the kindest thing.'

There are moments in our conversation when Grace smiles as other memories flicker to life, like nights in their grass house with six other girls, whispering in the dark – just like a regular sleepover. 'We'd be talking instead of sleeping,' Grace says. 'Those girls, some were killed in battle, some came back. So I think those are the good times we had together. We had some time to spare after a long day. We could sacrifice sleep and talk about silly stories, like being kids.'

On other nights her youthful exuberance was met with violence. On one particularly hot evening Grace and some other girls decided to sleep under the stars. 'We brought our mats to sleep out,' Grace says. 'I don't know why, but I started dancing.'

Soon all the girls were on their feet, shimmying and singing beneath the African sky. They didn't realise the LRA commanders were at that time trying to draw up battle plans for an assault. Around 11 pm a furious Lagony had his bed brought outside and ordered the girls to dance non-stop through the night. Whenever they stopped he flayed them with a cane. The poor children danced until sunrise.

Eventually, Lagony apologised to the seething Grace and promised never to cane her again. Her feisty stubbornness appeared to have grown on him. Deluded, he even imagined a ludicrous future when they would live happily ever after in a subterranean villa. 'Sometimes we would just sit and chat, and he said, "One day we'll overthrow the government. We're going to build our house under the ground so you have your office and no one sees you."'

Nearly four years after he forced Grace to become his 'wife', Otti Lagony was killed – shot by Joseph Kony, who believed he was plotting against him. 'In a strange way my abuser's death was hard for me,' says Grace. She had come to rely on him, whether she chose to or not. Being one of Lagony's wives had also given her protection as a sick counterweight to the child sexual abuse she endured. 'I had to be treated fairly and with respect by the other commanders,' Grace explains. 'They couldn't order me around at will or force me to carry unnecessarily heavy loads for long distances. But with Otti's death, all that was gone.'

Grace's reliance on Otti Lagony suggests an element of Stockholm syndrome – an expression used to describe the bonding of captives with their tormentors. The term originated after a 1973 bank robbery in Stockholm, Sweden, when four employees held hostage in the bank's vault for six days expressed sympathy for their captors. While not recognised as a psychiatric condition, Stockholm syndrome is seen as a survival mechanism. At any rate, Grace took all the help she could get.

There had been talk of killing her, too, but Kony decided to spare her. Three months later he allocated her to his chief of command, a man named Hodong. Not long afterwards, however, Kony sent Hodong across the border to fight in Uganda but instructed Grace to remain in Sudan, where her life of slavery continued.

Now around sixteen, Grace worked in hot, backbreaking conditions, farming for twelve hours a day. She still couldn't have pointed to her position on a map if she'd had one. With no end to her ordeal in sight, Grace fell back on her attitude of acceptance and focused purely on surviving.

I'm constantly struck by Grace's refusal to give up hope. At that stage she had spent one quarter of her life immersed in terror and untold suffering, and there seemed no end to it. How does someone so young find the will to keep going? As I try to wrap my head around it I'm reminded of Eddie Jaku's words in *The Happiest Man on Earth*:

'Tomorrow will come if you survive today. One step at a time.'

Grace enthusiastically agrees and says hope can be found in the most unlikely places – even in the scar tissue of suffering. 'Hope can come from seeing that every day people get injured, and even without medication they still get up and walk,' Grace declares, emphasising the point with a swift upward motion of her hands. 'They might have a disability, like one leg is shot or one hand is not there, but they're still alive and thankful that they didn't die! That gives a little bit of hope.'

In May 2001, Grace was left alone at the camp with a small group of girls when Kony and his soldiers left to carry out a raid. It was the chance she'd dreamed of for more than four years. After the men left Grace announced she was planning to escape. Because no one ever dared say that, on pain of death, few thought she was serious. Two girls, close friends of Grace, knew better. Nighty was a wife of Grace's new 'husband', Hodong, and Rose was the widow of a fallen LRA commander. Both had baby girls, both knew Grace was serious and both wanted in on her plan.

Their desperation and willingness tore at Grace. 'When I went to bed I was really anxious because I was thinking, "Is this a good idea? What if they kill these women? It will be all my fault. What if I leave them here? Because we're always together they might kill them anyway."'

Aware it was the only real chance to flee that had ever arisen, Grace knew they had to take it. 'Eventually I said, "We're leaving tomorrow night."'

Around 10 pm on 19 May 2001, the three girls crept to the edge of the camp. Rose and Nighty had wrapped their daughters in double layers of cloth in the hope they'd feel secure and less inclined to cry. Barefoot so they could walk in silence, the little escape party tiptoed to freedom. They waded through the river that meandered past the camp and trekked into the night, soon regretting their decision to leave their shoes behind.

Nighty and Rose said they knew the way to Juba, a major town in southern Sudan. When dawn arrived, however, the girls were horrified to realise they were almost back at the camp. For eight hours they'd walked in a giant circle. 'To be honest we didn't have a plan, which is stupid,' says Grace, throwing her head back to laugh. They'd zigzagged back and forth, not realising they were crossing the same river over and over again. 'At six am,' says Grace, 'we were back where we started.'

They all knew what that meant; just weeks earlier they'd been forced to watch as a teenage deserter was tied to a tree and beaten to death. Grace knew her death would be agonising. 'I've committed the biggest crime ever!' Grace remembers thinking as she crouched in the grass listening to voices from the camp. 'I've taken two women and two children, which the LRA claim are their future!'

The three girls held their breath as the voices drew near. Says Grace: 'I could hear someone saying, "I wonder where they've gone. I think we should start looking for them." I wasn't breathing, I swear I wasn't. I was holding my breath. And they pass.'

With the coast momentarily clear, Grace told the girls to run. They tore through the bush at speed for hours, cutting their feet to ribbons on the rough terrain. Ultimately their salvation rested on the fact they were in Sudan, where a civil war had been raging since 1983. 'The Sudanese government always had their soldiers up in the trees,' Grace explains. 'But I spotted them before they spotted us.'

After telling Rose and Nighty to hide in the bush, she approached the Sudanese soldiers, but not before adding, 'If they shoot me, run for your lives.'

With hands held above her head, Grace stepped slowly into the open. 'I don't have any gun,' she declared to the men in the trees. 'I just want to go to your boss. I escaped from our camp. Can you take me to your barracks?'

It was a life-and-death gamble. Rumour had it that the United Nations had done a deal with the Sudanese government, requesting they not return any captured rebels to the camps. Grace could only hope it was true. The soldiers climbed down and approached Grace with their guns drawn. Amazingly, says Grace, they agreed to help. 'I said, "I have my two other friends, can they come as well? They have children and they're a little bit scared so can you point your guns down?"'

Even when they arrived at the nearby Sudanese government barracks, Grace knew they weren't yet safe. The LRA were expert trackers and had no trouble hunting down escapees – especially a group of three. Grace implored the Sudanese troops to protect them.

The girls were ushered into a grass hut and only permitted outside at night to use the toilet. Just as Grace had feared, the LRA soon arrived and demanded to know where the deserters were. The Sudanese denied knowledge but Kony's henchmen stayed in the area for days, forcing the local soldiers to step up security. Five days later, the LRA finally withdrew, allowing the soldiers to relocate the girls to the town of Juba further north on the banks of the White Nile.

That night representatives from the United Nations Children's Fund (UNICEF) were contacted and took the girls to a safe house. It was the first time Grace had felt secure since she was twelve years old. 'When we got there it was a little bit like home,' she says with a heavy sigh. 'I could see the girls smiling a little bit.'

Next they were flown to the Sudanese capital of Khartoum where, at last, they could fully exhale. For two months, as the Ugandan government verified their identities, the girls savoured their newfound freedom. They explored the city, went to church, swam in the Nile and took the babies to the zoo. When it was time to return to Uganda, however, Grace was gripped by panic.

'I started crying and my heart skipped,' she says. 'I didn't want to go because it is unknown. I was really, *really* distressed.'

Grace, Nighty and Rose weren't the only lost souls who boarded the tense eight-hour flight back to Uganda. The plane was full of other former child soldiers, all contemplating their own fraught and confronting homecomings.

Their arrival at Entebbe Airport on 21 July 2001 made front-page news in Uganda. Government officials, journalists, photographers, families and a line of smiling female staff from World Vision were on hand to greet them. As Grace descended the steps to the tarmac she was overcome by a sense of terror. 'Where are we going?' she fretted inwardly. 'Are they going to take us to jail?'

The girls and babies were bundled into a car with women from World Vision. 'There was total silence,' Grace remembers, cutting the air with a chop of her hand. 'I was just so scared and I felt my heart beating really fast. The ladies were offering us some water and asking, "Is there any type of music you like to listen to?" But we didn't drink.'

Five years and four months of brainwashing had erased the girls' innocence. Joseph Kony had always warned that any escapees would eventually be found and poisoned. In the girls' minds, the smiling World Vision women and their bottles of water posed a lethal threat.

Grace was still silent eight hours later when the car arrived at World Vision's Children of War Rehabilitation Centre near her home patch in Gulu. But soon her guard came down – if only a little. Surveying the great throng of other rescued children gathered at the centre she felt the faint beginnings of a sense of belonging. 'There were so many kids and everybody was singing!' Grace recalls with a wide-eyed expression. 'I said, "I know this person! They haven't killed him! I know *most* of these people!"'

Grace was shocked to realise how many kids she'd grown up with had also been snatched from their village. Then a lump formed in her throat when she spied her cousin

David – long rumoured to have been killed by the LRA – among the dancing horde. 'I remember a sense of relief,' Grace says softly. 'I could feel a little bit safe.'

While some children returned to their homes, Grace remained in the rehabilitation centre for five months. She felt more secure in Gulu than in her village, the scene of so many abductions. Her mum, too, was nervous about Grace's return, fearing the LRA might come for her. One day Grace received a visit from Florence, a childhood friend. When Florence mentioned she'd just finished senior school and was planning to study nursing, a spark fired in Grace's mind, suddenly reigniting her childhood passion for education. She marched straight to the centre manager.

'I was crying and said, "I want to go to school! I just want to *be someone*,"' Grace remembers.

The local school agreed to take Grace but, since she hadn't been in a classroom for five years, she was encouraged to refresh at primary school first. 'I was quite a sight,' she says, laughing loudly. 'I was a gangly seventeen-year-old in class with much younger children.'

Conveniently the school was across the street from the rehabilitation centre, and when Grace wasn't studying she did what she could to help the flow of broken new arrivals from Kony's crazed war. Around fifteen former child soldiers came through the doors every day, having escaped or been rescued. 'I would help the children feel at ease,' says Grace. 'It's a little bit scary. I was scared as well, but I was okay.'

Due to the LRA's nomadic existence many children who wound up in Gulu were thousands of kilometres from their homes. Some had even crossed international borders. As Grace already knew, not all families welcomed their long-lost children. Some were superstitious, believing them to be evil or diseased, while others feared a visit from the LRA.

Rehabilitation of a child soldier is slow, intense and challenging. Many had witnessed extreme brutality and been forced to participate in ritual murder. Girls had endured years of rape. Some were pregnant while others – like Nighty and Rose – were already mothers. The boys were often violent, proud of their military service and nostalgic for the prestige and power a gun had once given them. On top of the mental injuries, many required medical attention for wounds that had been crudely dealt with on the battlefield and never properly healed. Those still young enough for school could return to study. Older survivors were taught skills and trades.

'I count myself as among the lucky people,' says Grace. 'I have people who contributed towards my recovery and they don't even know me, but they've made a great difference. That's why I am who I am today.'

A year after her salvation Grace enrolled as a boarder at St Mary's College in Aboke, 75 kilometres south-east of Gulu. It was the same school where the LRA's abduction of 139 students had made international headlines just five years earlier, but the giant front gates made Grace feel secure. After graduating from high school – and inspired by the counsellors who'd helped her rehabilitate – Grace enrolled at Gulu University to study social work.

After she gained her degree, she took a job with World Vision, helping other former child soldiers readjust to life. It was not an easy task: Grace says most were still at war internally and many were in physical pain from old wounds. But she knew better than most how important it was to put aside the evil of the LRA and to dig down to the traumatised children buried beneath the human wreckage they had created. For Grace, the desire to help is innate. 'I like to help people,' she says easily. 'Even when someone has done me bad I think they probably didn't know what they were doing. They're probably going through something.'

In 2011 a new chapter in Grace's life opened when she moved to Sydney with the help of a World Vision sponsorship. She was initially granted a protection visa, before becoming an Australian citizen. Keen to add to her studies,

Grace focused on early-childhood intervention and today holds a bachelor's degree in social work from the University of Sydney. 'Everyone is treated equally, regardless of background,' she says of her life in Australia. 'The community and government were welcoming, there is welfare to support people in need or unable to work, and human rights are protected better than in Uganda. I haven't had any bad experiences.'

She is, however, surprised by the level of homelessness in the largest, glistening city of our very rich country.

Although it's believed Joseph Kony is still alive, the LRA has withered from three thousand members to around one hundred soldiers today. They were all but expelled from Uganda by the end of 2006. The International Criminal Court issued arrest warrants for Kony and his commanders, indicting them for war crimes and crimes against humanity.

As the LRA's reign of terror faded, the Gulu rehab centre closed for good in 2013. 'I feel sorry for the children who came after the closure,' says Grace. 'They don't have anyone to walk them towards their recovery. Most of the NGOs were doing that work and because there's no active war at the moment in Uganda, they've moved to other places. So this is a time that people really need that and they don't have it.'

Grace says the problem is exacerbated by the tendency in many African cultures not to share personal problems. 'There are young adults who have a really sad story and they haven't shared it with anyone!' she marvels.

As we talk about the importance of interpersonal communication the words of Eddie Jaku come to mind:

'Shared sorrow is half sorrow; shared pleasure is double pleasure.'

'I feel sharing helps you to lessen the burden,' Grace agrees. 'And that's why I'm who I am today, because I've shared with many people and I've had so many people listen to my story and it's helped. But there are people who have it all in their head burning, and every day they have nightmares. They have no one to turn to.'

This is a void Grace hopes to help fill. She has established her own foundation – Bedo Ki Gen (Ugandan for 'living with hope') – with the aim of building a new rehab centre in Gulu. 'I want someone to be there to listen to survivors,' she says. 'And if you need help you have somewhere to go. Because someone being there to listen, I feel like it was the most important part of who I am today.'

Just as Tonya Whitwell tapped into a unique vein of empathy by communicating with survivors she found on Gold Coast park benches, Grace is able to reach children who have endured the same horrors she once faced.

Paradoxically she is grateful her experiences gave her a unique perspective and a powerful reach.

Today Grace lives a busy life in Sydney, where she works with disabled children under the age of six. It's challenging and emotionally draining but she is happy she's having a positive impact. Her private life is not without challenges either. While Grace is engaged to be married, her fiancé, Richard – an accountant with the Ugandan Customs Department – remains in Africa as their wedding was put on hold by the pandemic. When it does happen, they'll have a civil wedding in Australia and a traditional ceremony in Uganda. Then Grace plans to go back to university. 'I'm still dreaming,' she says. 'I've always wanted to work for the UN Women's League or World Vision International. I have to do my master's so I'm looking at project management.'

COVID has also had an impact on her mental health, with lockdowns sparking memories of her former isolation. 'My life as a teenager was pretty much like living under lockdown, with nowhere to go and no one to turn to but my abusers,' she says. 'I call that time the Dark Age.' But her biggest fears were reserved for the vulnerable children living in violent homes, and young girls forced into marriage by desperate families.

When I ask Grace what she considers key to her survival and her blossoming future, I'm not surprised to hear echoes of Tonya Whitwell. 'Acceptance for me is always the first step of any situation,' says Grace. 'It doesn't matter what kind of a situation you are in – accept you have more strength, you have more strategy to deal with it. If you keep fighting it, you won't survive long. Then you hope this will change with time.'

Grace's strongest advice, however, is to never give up. 'I think when you're knocked down, always get up and keep moving,' she says. 'And then you look at a way forward. Looking to the future is hope. It doesn't mean I don't have flashbacks and that I don't sit and cry. I'm a very emotional person. I cry most of the time! But you can still pick life. You can decide who you want to be. I choose to be happy.'

Spoken like someone who has lived one hundred years.

Three

Juli

I had no idea my friend was a raging alcoholic. No one did. In fact Juli Ogilvy's life had always looked like a particularly sunny place to me. Married to a world-class golfer, she had an access-all-areas pass to every privilege the A-list had to offer: year-round travel, first-class seats, red-carpet events, five-star hotels and the opportunity to rub shoulders with the rich, powerful and famous. It never entered my head that hers could be a lonely world of pain and self-destruction.

We first met at a golf tournament in Coolum, Queensland, in December 2006. At the time my husband, John, was working for the Professional Golfers' Association (PGA) and her husband, Geoff Ogilvy, was one of the event's star attractions. The tournament was one of the few on the calendar where players mixed business and pleasure – most of them brought their wives and children. We'd gather in the evening sun after play had finished for woodfired pizzas as the kids ran amok.

I found Juli to be fabulous company: intelligent, warm and funny. Her bubbly personality glistened from behind a set of dazzling blue eyes and a beautiful smile. She seemed to be 'living the dream'.

Fast forward to 2010 and Juli had three babies under the age of four. The demands of domestic life had yanked her off the glamorous merry-go-round of the PGA Tour and now a more mundane and isolated existence was underway – for her at least. While Juli slogged it out at home, exhausted and knee-deep in nappies, Geoff continued to strut the world stage they used to dance upon together.

Feeling increasingly ostracised and resentful, Juli looked around for a distraction, which slowly morphed into a chemical ritual as she tried to flatten waves of emotional pain that welled up inside her. It started with a glass of wine and could easily have ended in her death.

For years the world around her continued to turn, oblivious to the silent crisis unfolding in Juli's life. Then, in October 2017, she finally sent up a distress flare. I was absently thumbing through my social media feed when I saw it – her open letter to the universe.

'I am an alcoholic . . .' it began.

Those four words stopped me in my tracks. They made me cry for Juli but they made me so proud of her, too. I told her I'd be honoured if she one day allowed me to share her story.

It was eight minutes to midnight on Sunday 30 April 2017 when Juli teetered on the brink of a life-altering moment. She'd collapsed into bed having drunk a bottle of wine, a bottle of champagne and an entire bottle of vodka, with only her demons for company. Even by her steadily dropping standards it was an appalling amount. As the room spun out of control Juli pulled out her phone and managed to snap a photo of her bedside alarm clock – showing 11.52 pm – and wondered whether she'd drink on the plane the next morning.

'This will be your last drink ever,' she promised herself as the deviant thought entered her head.

'No!' her demons snapped. 'Who cares if you show up drunk? You're already a drunk!'

The morning would bring the first of May – the date Juli had chosen to begin her recovery. She'd booked herself on a flight from her home in Phoenix, Arizona, to stay with her mother in Texas to dry out. By the time the alarm tore her from inebriated sleep, a fundamental shift had occurred. There would be no drinking on the plane.

'I woke up that morning knowing I had to change my life,' Juli tells me. 'Something in me just said, "Girl, you've got to save yourself. You've just *got* to."'

Salvation had been a long time coming. The celebrity stratosphere where she once soared was a long way from the tumbleweeds and longhorn cattle of Dimmitt, a tiny smudge of a town in the north-western corner of Texas where Juli Justice was born in 1976. Dimmitt boasted one set of traffic lights and a population of 4000, mostly comprised of cowboys in ten-gallon hats and pick-up trucks.

Four years later her parents, Jasper and Janet Justice, moved with Juli and her sister, Jennifer, to the larger Texan town of Paris. There were more traffic lights there, more people, and a one-tenth-scale replica of the Eiffel Tower topped with a giant red cowboy hat on the outskirts of town.

Janet was a schoolteacher and once appeared on the TV quiz show *Jeopardy!*, while Jasper was the deacon at their local First Baptist Church. Devout Christians, the Justices worshipped every Wednesday and twice on Sundays. Jasper also worked as a realtor and was governed by God in every way. Honest and charitable, he was so devoted to finding clients the perfect home he'd sell them his own if it met their needs. Juli says they moved five times before she was in third grade.

Juli was the image of her dad: blonde hair, blue eyes, a dimple on her cheek, a wicked sense of humour and a quick mind. 'We were two peas in a pod, best friends,' she tells me with a smile during one of our many chats over Zoom. 'I went to him for everything.'

His cancer diagnosis in 1990 was a crushing blow to thirteen-year-old Juli. She remembers their last Thanksgiving dinner together a year or so later. 'He sat at the table and he looked like hell,' she continues quietly. 'He was as white as your shirt and his eyes were sunken in. He was so thin. Then he said he needed to go to the hospital and I knew at that moment he wasn't coming home.'

A few days later the family gathered at his bedside to say goodbye. 'He was on morphine and I remember my grandmother kept saying, "It's okay to let go. It's okay to let go."'

It was meant to comfort, but Juli was aghast. 'I kept thinking, "How could she say that? How could she tell him it's okay?"'

Jasper's death at forty-four had a massive impact on Juli. She's still unpacking it today, thirty years later. Haunted by the image of her father in an open casket, Juli remembers people trying to soothe her with variations of 'You'll see him again in heaven'. Like that would somehow fix things. Juli needed him here on earth as her fifteenth year went from bad to worse. A few months after she lost her dad, her first boyfriend broke her heart. And just one day after her sixteenth birthday, Juli's beloved paternal grandfather passed away, too.

The death of a parent is one of the worst traumas a child can face. Indeed, parental loss is among the most emotionally difficult and universal human experiences, no matter what age we are. According to the Australian Bureau of Statistics, one in twenty Australian children will experience the death of a parent before they turn eighteen. It's usually the first time they experience grief, and they will most likely lack any coping mechanisms. When a child is robbed of someone so significant, they often define their life in terms of 'before' the death and 'after'.

'Experiencing the death of a loved parent in early life has the potential to increase the young person's vulnerability to anxiety and depression, and to decrease self-esteem,' says Dianne McKissock, one of the founders of the National Centre for Childhood Grief.

During the mid-teen years, when it's so important to fit in with our peers, grieving can set a child apart. There's a risk of being labelled 'the kid whose dad died'. Those who have lost a parent may feel people are watching to see how they're coping, and anxious when they don't know how to act. They may also worry about day-to-day things like family structure, living arrangements and finances. Impacts will vary depending on which parent has died. In Juli's case, it was the one she relied on the most – her protector and comforter.

'I know I have him on a pedestal,' Juli tells me, her voice emotional, 'but I'm realistic, too. He just was the most beautiful man. He was my ally in the house.'

According to the *Journal of the Royal Society of Medicine*, children who experience parental loss are more prone to mental health issues, reduced academic success, lower self-esteem and risky sexual behaviour. Girls who lose their dads can also add unwise relationship choices, eating disorders and substance abuse to that heartbreaking list. And so it was with Juli.

The emotional ties to her church that had once made her feel safe were now strangling her. Juli abandoned structure and scripture for parties, drinking and boys. She was already on a slippery slope when a twenty-one-year-old family friend took advantage of her when she was sixteen years old. After hours and when no one was around, he enticed her down to the grounds of her former school and they had sex on the front steps.

Ashamed and confused, Juli was mortified when her soon-to-be stepsister told everyone about the 'encounter'. Having lost control over her privacy, her pain and her dignity, Juli wanted to claw back some ownership. 'When someone feels like they have no control over their life, what they can control is what goes into their bodies,' she explains. And so began her secret life of vomiting after meals.

The eating disorder bulimia nervosa is characterised by intense bingeing episodes followed by purging (vomiting) and/or overexercising. The causes are complex but can be broken down into four general categories: biological factors such as genetics; developmental factors, including our personalities and childhood trauma; psychological factors such as mental illness; and sociocultural factors such as our obsession with being thin.

Juli says she ticked two of those boxes: developmental trauma and a sociocultural obsession. 'It was me looking in the mirror and thinking, "I feel gross and fat,"' she admits. Purging, she adds, made her feel like she was back in command. 'I can remember the first time I did it,' she says. 'It was like I had just shot myself up with drugs. It felt so good to purge. To get it out.'

Typically bulimics find their disorder ebbs and flows. It may abate for long periods before being reignited by stress, sometimes years down the track. This was precisely Juli's experience. The trigger for her relapse came at a party during her first year studying restaurant and hotel management at Texas Tech University.

All the freshman girls at Texas Tech had their eye on 'Finn', one of the college jocks. Good-looking and athletic, he oozed charm and confidence. One night he asked Juli to a party at the home of a friend whose parents were out of town. Juli was nervous but thrilled to be by Finn's side at the boozy bash and, when she joined him for a short drive to get cigarettes, he kissed her in the car. 'I remember being so excited,' Juli says. 'I thought, "This guy's into me and he's so cute!"'

Late in the night after having too much to drink, Juli crawled into bed at the house alone. She and Finn were sharing a room and she tells me she might even have considered sex with him if she hadn't been so intoxicated. 'I passed out but then I woke up and he was inside me, on top of me, from behind,' she says, her Texan drawl laced with sadness. 'I just kept saying, "No, no, no, Finn! Not like this! I'm too drunk!" And he just kept going.'

Shame and awkwardness silenced Juli as they drove back to college the next morning. She knew the encounter wasn't normal or healthy but she blamed herself. 'I was drunk,' she says. 'And so I carried that shame with me.'

They didn't speak again for six weeks until Finn called her out of the blue. 'There was a party for my sorority and everyone wanted to go,' Juli remembers. 'He didn't have a date and he said, "I'd love to go with you." I was nineteen and I look back now and think what a dumbass I was because I should have known he was using me again. But I thought, "Maybe it wasn't what I thought it was. Maybe it wasn't rape?"'

She agreed to go to the party with him, and when they went back to another friend's house that weekend, she had sex with him. This consensual second encounter left her even more confused by making her re-evaluate the first. 'I thought that I wasn't raped because I'd slept with him again,' she says.

Deep down the undeniable truth gnawed at her. In the hope of disgorging the guilt and shame, Juli started to vomit in secret again. It would be another twenty-five years before she recognised her first night with Finn for what it was.

The moment came in 2018 as she watched news coverage detailing allegations of sexual assault levelled at Brett Kavanaugh, a senior jurist who'd been nominated to the US Supreme Court by then president Donald Trump. Christine Blasey Ford – an eminent professor of psychology – claimed Kavanaugh had sexually attacked her at a party when she was fifteen. Professor Blasey Ford said

Kavanaugh was drunk, and had restrained her and tried to force himself on her.

Kavanaugh denied the claims (and now sits on the US Supreme Court), but Juli says the case opened an emotional floodgate inside her. 'I cried for days hearing Christine Blasey Ford give her testimony,' she says.

Overwhelmed and unable to escape her thoughts, Juli finally opened up about the rape she suffered as a teenager with her therapist. Her therapist had known what had happened but had been waiting for Juli to feel ready to confront it. 'It was the first time that I had ever told the story top to toe,' she says.

Even today Juli says she still carries shame about being raped. When I ask her why and point out it wasn't her fault, she sighs. 'Because I let him have sex with me again,' she says. 'That's the part of rape that people don't understand. The shame women put on themselves is worse than anything else.'

When Juli was nineteen, her sister, Jennifer, stumbled upon her eating disorder. 'We had a sandwich by the pool and I went back to our little condo to vomit and there was a piece of lettuce left in the toilet,' Juli confesses. 'My sister saw it and knew what I was doing immediately. She sat me down and said, "I love you and we can't have this happen. Do you want to tell Mum or do you want me to?"'

Juli cringingly told her mother she was bulimic and soon informed a therapist, too. Although her condition improved with counselling, Juli's tumultuous years were far from over. At twenty-one, a night out with a friend led to more heartbreak. 'We found ourselves chatting all night at a bar,' Juli says. 'He'd just buried his best friend a month before and had been one of the guys who'd found him – he'd shot himself in their share house. He was in a very dark place when we met.'

She slept with her friend that night and fell pregnant. Frightened and dismayed, Juli felt she couldn't tell anyone about it. She eventually looked for support in the *Yellow Pages*. She phoned an organisation that looked like it could help her and asked if they supported abortion. When the person at the other end of the line assured her they did, Juli made an appointment to see them. When she turned up at their offices a few days later, however, she found herself in an emotional ambush. 'They put me in a room and left me alone to watch a video of a baby, the same size mine would have been, and it had a heartbeat,' Juli remembers. 'I couldn't get out of there fast enough.'

Her next call was to Planned Parenthood, where she was met with tenderness and counselled about all of her options. She booked in for her procedure a few days later and was thankful when her boyfriend agreed to go with her. 'He took me there, with all the protesters yelling at us and throwing their pictures in my face,' Juli recalls. 'It was awful. But once inside it was this beautiful room of women, all strangers, but going through the worst day of our lives together.'

Juli recognised a couple of girls she vaguely knew from around town. 'We never spoke of it afterward,' she says, 'but we always gave each other hugs when we saw one another. An unspoken bond.'

We talk for a while about abortion and the social stigma that can come with it, particularly in America's so-called Bible Belt, where Juli was raised. As the daughter of a Baptist deacon she knows better than most the dogmatic pressure that can be applied to young women who unwittingly fall pregnant.

In June 2022, the US Supreme Court overturned *Roe v. Wade* – the 1973 ruling that recognised a woman's constitutional right to an abortion. At the time of writing, abortion is about to become illegal in potentially half of America.

'It makes me so angry!' says Juli as we finally catch up for dinner.

Juli says she's glad she had the legal right in Texas, and maintains the abortion was the best decision for her and her boyfriend. 'My reasons are personal,' she says. 'A woman should never have to explain her "why" for terminating a pregnancy. It's her body. It's her heart. It's her decision and she alone has to live with it.'

That's not to say the experience left her emotionally unscarred. Echoes of that time dwelt deep in her subconscious. 'Not long after, I had a dream,' she recalls. 'My dad and grandfather came to me in a hospital room. They were holding hands and smiling. My dad reached down and picked up a navy-blue baby carrier and said, "It's okay. We've got him." And then they left.'

It remains the only time her dad has ever talked to her in a dream.

Upon graduating from college in 1999 at twenty-three, Juli enrolled in culinary school in Arizona – 2000 kilometres from home, far enough away to promise her a fresh start. With her bulimia under control she felt like she could close the door on the torment of her teenage years.

As Juli didn't know a soul in Phoenix, her mum gave her the number of some old family friends, Danny and Kim. They had five kids and needed a babysitter. It wasn't long before Juli became part of the family and fell in with their social circle, too. Among them were an Australian pro golfer and his wife, who decided to play matchmaker and introduced Juli to a friend of theirs who'd just moved to the US. He was Geoff Ogilvy, a twenty-two-year-old Australian golfer in his rookie year on the PGA Tour. Juli fell hard and fast for the charming 6'2" Aussie. 'He was living large and feeling great,' Juli remembers fondly.

Their relationship went from zero to one hundred very fast. 'We met in May and I quit my job to come to Australia for six weeks in December!' Juli says with a laugh. 'His sister got married the second week, so I met his whole family super quick.'

Pro golfers spend ten months of the year travelling the globe as the PGA's glittering caravan rolls from one spectacular venue to the next. That amount of time away would put a strain on any relationship, let alone a new one, so instead of returning to a full-time job in Arizona, Juli joined Geoff on the road and in the skies. Within a few years they'd married.

'We just loved each other and soaked each other up,' she says. 'I fit right in with his family, with his friends and the golf world. We had all these great friends that were couples, and we were all young and travelling the world. It was pretty brilliant.'

Their relationship bloomed in tandem with Geoff's form on the golf course. His first PGA Tour win came in 2005, three months after he and Juli tied the knot in Phoenix. He won a sudden-death play-off to take out the Chrysler Classic in Tucson, Arizona. 'People play for twenty years and never win a tournament profession-ally,' Juli exclaims. 'It's a big deal. I can just remember feeling that day . . . "Oh my god, he's done it! This is life-changing!"'

Geoff's next win was at the 2006 US Open – one of the big four tournaments that make up the annual 'majors'. A heatwave blasted New York as Juli, five months pregnant with their first child, struggled to push through the crowds at the Winged Foot Golf Club. Geoff had played an incred-ible round but was on the fringes of a close tussle between American star Phil Mickelson and Scottish player Colin Montgomerie. The gallery held its breath as Geoff chipped in from off the green on the seventeenth hole, but at the final hole the silence was broken by a shrieking Juli. 'It's all quiet except, on the footage, you can hear me scream and I'm just freaking out,' she says with a chortle. 'I thought, "Holy shit! My husband's gonna finish second or third in a major!"'

In one of the wildest finishes in US Open history, Mickelson and Montgomerie both double-bogeyed the final hole (taking two more strokes to reach the hole than they should) to give Geoff the win and instantly propel him to number eight in the world. 'It will always be one of the best memories ever, *ever*, of my life,' says Juli. 'That day, being so proud of him, so proud for proving it to everyone.'

The young couple could not have been riding higher. It was a fairytale victory that rocketed them to even greater heights. Their firstborn, Phoebe, arrived four months later and slipped nicely into the nomadic sports star lifestyle. 'She was in Hawaii at five weeks old, Australia at seven weeks and back in Hawaii at nine weeks old,' says Juli. 'We took her everywhere!' A son, Jasper, joined them fifteen months later but he was a little less enamoured of jetsetting, or even settling most days. 'Jasper just cried and cried and cried, and it just about broke me,' says Juli. 'I think Geoff will tell you that going from zero children to one was hard for him. Well, going from one child to two was my worst transition. That rocked me.'

The Department of Health says as many as one in five mums develop postnatal depression. Research has also shown it's often the arrival of a second child that increases the risk. 'The increased time pressure associated with second births explains mothers' worse mental health,' concluded a study by Leah Ruppanner, Francisco Perales and Janeen Baxter published in the American *Journal of Marriage and Family.*

When Jasper was three months old, Juli was diagnosed with postnatal depression and prescribed antidepressants.

Geoff had returned to the Tour by then so they hired a nanny to help shuttle their growing family around the world. Somehow they managed to pull it off until baby number three – an adorable bundle named Harvey – joined them two years later.

I can't imagine the stress of getting six people – three of them babies – on and off twenty flights all year round. Then there's the ground-transport logistics, highchairs in hotel rooms, feeding times and sleeping arrangements. The mind boggles. Juli's certainly did. In the end they gave up and decided she should settle with the kids in Del Mar, California, while Geoff continued on the Tour alone.

Any mum will tell you how tough those first few years can be. Mine were an ordeal, too. When I was hosting *Sunrise* I'd get up at 2.30 am to feed my baby before starting work at 4 am. But Juli was also struggling with postnatal depression and now had to juggle three very young children without her husband for much of the time. Exhausted, and desperately missing Geoff, she felt resentment start to rear its head as she watched him living the high life from afar. 'I was jealous that he got to be alone, that he got to go out to dinner and I was – I don't want to say stuck – but I was constantly with our kids. I didn't leave them. Ever.'

The pressure of their unconventional lives grew steadily worse. Juli and Geoff struggled to communicate and his form at work hit a rough patch, too. 'He just shut me out completely,' says Juli. 'I couldn't talk to him about what was going on because he'd say, "You don't understand." I was afraid if I rocked the boat it would make his golf even worse. He was like this fragile piece of art that I had to keep safe and not disturb.'

I remember my own feelings of isolation as a new mum too well: home all day with just Oprah Winfrey for company, dirty nappies piling up and the smell of milk throughout the house. My son, Nick, would only sleep for about twenty minutes during the day if I held him, so my husband would come home from work to find me sitting in the dark, too afraid to turn the light on lest I wake up the baby.

But at least I could get out and about to my mothers' group, or just to playgroups in the local park. Women who gave birth during 2020 and 2021 had a whole extra layer on top of the isolation that caring for a newborn brings. A study by Curtin University found higher-than-normal levels of stress and anxiety in both parents and medical practitioners during the pandemic. It's understandable: visitors were banned from hospitals, at times partners couldn't be present for births, antenatal education was conducted via telehealth and follow-ups with lactation consultants via phone, borders were shut and family members were unable to visit each other, and health restrictions kept new parents from their support networks. The impact on the celebratory side of parenting was as harsh as on the practical side. After all, introducing your newborn to everyone is one of life's joys.

Many women quietly admit to losing their identity when they first have a child. Our varied and vibrant lives can be unwittingly whittled down by friends, colleagues and even well-meaning family members to fit into a narrow pigeonhole – 'new mum'. Of course, that's only part of the picture, and every woman is different. Having a baby brings so many immeasurable positives, but I think we have to acknowledge it can also herald loss and change – for your relationships, independence, job, social life, leisure, spontaneity and confidence. Some women, of course, reach for a crutch.

Research out of the US has looked at the correlation between elevated alcohol consumption and postpartum depression. It estimates that up to 15 per cent of new mothers are affected by postpartum depression and, of those, 15 per cent self-medicate by binge drinking.

Australia's National Health and Medical Research Council defines binge drinking as the consumption of five or more standard drinks in a night. For heavy drinking it's even more. Alcohol abuse is the dependency on alcohol to reduce or eliminate one's emotional, mental or spiritual dissatisfaction. Juli was quickly slipping into the abuse category.

In the evening, she chose to 'take the edge off' with a glass of wine. It was only one drink and it was easy to justify: 'I've got three kids, I can have a glass of wine!' But all too soon it became two glasses, until – over the space of twelve months – it was two bottles. 'I'd pick the kids up from school at three pm, I'd pour my first drink at three-thirty pm and I'd drink until I went to bed, without stopping,' she says.

With Geoff travelling between twenty-seven and thirty weeks a year, I ask Juli if he ever said anything when he was home. 'Oh, he'd say things like, "I'm going to do dry July" or "I'm going to do dry January" or "I'm going to take a couple weeks off from drinking,"' Juli replies. 'I'd say, "You go for it! Do your thing, but I'm not stopping!"'

By the time Harvey turned three, Juli was draining two bottles of wine a day. The more she drank, the heavier she got, so she switched to vodka in a woefully misguided weight-loss regime. As a bonus she also figured people would be less likely to smell it. 'I functioned beautifully as an alcoholic,' she says. 'No one knew.'

Socially, Juli's drinking didn't raise any eyebrows. 'We'd have all these mum nights out and my group of friends in Arizona all partied quite a bit,' she remembers. 'So they just thought I was like them! I would always be the last one standing, having a great time dancing and drinking until the cows came home. I was just a good-time girl.'

None of her friends, however, had any idea she was drunk all day, every day. When Juli says she 'functioned beautifully' as an alcoholic, she's alluding to functional alcoholism. A functional alcoholic is dependent on alcohol but can still go about their daily activities with a level of competence. The Hazelden Betty Ford Foundation describes someone 'who *appears* to have their drinking and behaviour relatively under control. They might drink too much or too often, but they seem to be doing fairly well in various areas despite possible substance abuse. People often look at social standards of success and mistakenly believe that a person is "functioning" or doesn't truly have an alcohol use disorder.'

They may appear physically and mentally healthy, but struggle with uncontrollable cravings and obsessive thoughts about their next drink. Typically they are well-educated and have stable jobs and families. Functional alcoholics are often in denial of the problem, usually because they haven't encountered any sharply negative consequences such as an arrest, or a financial hit. They can also develop an elevated tolerance for alcohol, so it takes more for them to feel the effects, and therefore they need to drink more to get the desired effect.

I ask Juli if she has any idea how much she was spending on alcohol.

'About $7000 a year,' she says. Over five years she spent US$35,000 – that's close to AUD$50,000. 'And alcohol is much cheaper in America than it is in Australia,' she points out.

Juli's family knew she drank a lot, but she kept them in the dark about exactly *how* much by virtue of the fact her mum and sister still lived in Texas. 'They'd come to town or I'd go see them and I was getting hammered but they didn't see it day in and day out,' she says.

High functioning or not, there were nights when Juli had no idea what happened or how she got into bed. By 2015 she was downing a bottle of vodka every night of the week. With that much alcohol in her bloodstream, she required a couple of shots of vodka in the morning just to stop the shakes and 'feel normal'.

Clearly her tragic self-poisoning was unsustainable. Mercifully, rock bottom was racing up to meet her. For Juli's fortieth birthday the Ogilvys and three other couples rented a house in Mexico. Late one night, drunk on champagne, vodka, tequila and wine, she erupted.

'Everything I had been feeling for a long time just went boom!' she says. Anger, resentment, loneliness. 'All the festering just came out. The things that I spewed were truthful, it's just that when you are an alcoholic and you spew your truth, a lot of people don't listen to it because they just see the ugly. They look at you with pity and I think that's how everyone saw me that night.'

The next morning was a dark place for Juli. 'I felt so much shame,' she recalls. 'I thought, "Why am I here? It's probably better for everyone that I'm not." I was hanging on by a thread.' An emotional rasp in Juli's voice betrays the pain and sorrow she still feels about having stood on the brink of suicide. 'Had I not had three children,' she says, 'I think I would have killed myself that next day.'

Juli was as low as she'd ever been, but she didn't hit true rock bottom until a few months later. After a night out with her girlfriends while the nanny at home looked after the kids, she stumbled outside a bar and struggled to remain upright as she waited for an Uber. On the trip home she had one of those 'solve the problems of the world' conversations with her driver that continued for an hour and a half after he'd pulled up outside her house. They talked about the war in Syria, and their families, and she even casually invited him and his wife to come for dinner sometime.

In the bleakness of another hungover morning, Juli sat with her head in her hands, aghast at the thought she'd drunkenly invited a perfect stranger into her children's home. 'The guilt that I put on myself after that night is just . . .' Juli trails off, struggling to find a strong enough word. 'No one could put more guilt on me,' she says finally. 'No one.'

Despite all the flashing signs, the frightening moments and dark thoughts, Juli tells me she was still in denial at this point. She refused to say the word alcoholic. But she says she knew deep down she had a problem.

She eventually decided to speak to a therapist, a gentle way to start addressing what was going on. Juli began weekly sessions, but even so she only dipped her toe into the notion of sobriety. 'I thought I could just cut down on my drinking,' she says. 'It worked for a while but, damn, that shit just crept back in and we decided it was time for me to get sober.'

The thought terrified her. 'I remember sitting in that session thinking, "I'm going to die! I'm going to *die*! It's just going to kill me. How the fuck am I going to live without alcohol? Do I even *want* to live without it?"'

In her heart, though, she knew the bottle was going to kill her anyway, one way or the other. That day she picked her sober date, 1 May 2017. Then she had to tell her family. 'Two of the hardest phone calls that I've ever made,' she says quietly. Juli called her mum and her sister back home in Texas, finally admitting how bad her drinking was and asking if she could come and stay to dry out. 'The shame I felt,' she tells me. 'I could hardly talk. I hated myself so much for letting them down.'

The night before her flight, however, on 30 April – with Geoff away playing in a tournament – she went on one stupefying final bender, capturing the last minutes of her last drunken day on her mobile phone: 11.52 pm.

With the nanny minding the kids, Juli arrived at her mum's place in Lubbock, Texas, feeling sick, burnt out and fearful – but sober. 'I felt like shit. I remember thinking, "I wish they could just put me in the hospital and knock me out for six months."' Having been in therapy, however, she knew she had to face the music and 'do the work'. If not for herself, then at least for her children. 'I didn't want to look at those three beautiful babies and have them think their mom died because she was an alcoholic,' she says.

There are two main ways to treat alcohol withdrawal – as an inpatient in a clinic or as an outpatient, with or without medication. Alcohol withdrawal can cause serious illness and even be fatal. The most acute symptoms tend to occur in the first six hours to four days from the last drink. They are short-lived for most people but can include sweating, tremors, hallucinations, brain fog, anxiety and fatigue. Seizures and/or the DTs (alcohol withdrawal delirium) occur in up to one of five patients.

Juli chose to go through withdrawal at home with the help of her family and her therapist. She says she wanted to sober up in the real world rather than the safe haven of a rehab facility. 'I needed to prove to myself that I can live day to day,' she explains.

In the days before she left to dry out at her mother's home, Juli told her closest girlfriends where she was going and why. 'I didn't want it to be a secret, for some reason,' she says. 'Maybe I wanted accountability for myself or maybe to help me when I did come back and face the real world.'

They armed her with a few key items for the weeks ahead – books, sweets, melatonin, messages of love and hope, 'and some dark and twisted drinking humour,' says Juli. 'I did know that I would have to find a way to laugh about it all.'

Janet Justice was waiting at the airport when her daughter arrived in Texas crying and ashamed, but Juli says her mum was simply proud of her. At first Juli slept most of the time; it was easier than being awake and wanting to die. 'I felt so exhausted,' Juli remembers. 'I think I slept for twelve hours that first night. I woke the next day about lunchtime and went back to bed. I remember lying there crying for a long while, thinking that sleep would help me escape the desire for death.' She wasn't suicidal, she just didn't want to feel – anything. 'It was coming down hard and fast and I couldn't numb anymore,' she says.

On day three Juli dragged herself out of bed to shower and get dressed.

She hung out with her family, cooked and even attempted some retail therapy. 'We went into this shop and they offered us a glass of wine,' she recalls. 'I was three days sober and we just started laughing. "I've come here to dry out! I'm drying out as we speak!"'

Janet had stocked the fridge with juice and Juli's favourite foods. They ordered takeaway when she had cravings, sat outside together in the sun, and talked when she needed but felt safe in silence when she didn't. 'It was hard to admit that I needed help in the first place, let alone that I needed my mom at forty years of age to dry out,' Juli says. 'And I needed her like I've never needed her before. My sister as well, and my stepdad. They cried with me and for me. They asked what they could do. I knew I wasn't alone even though I felt alone in my darkness that week. It was hell inside my head.'

It was one thing to be sober and vulnerable with her mum and sister, but when she flew home after a week in their care, Juli was scared to face the real world. She didn't know who she would be without the false bravado of booze. Would she even be herself? 'I thought, "How am I going to live?"' she says. '"How am I going to talk to people?" It had been so long since I hadn't had alcohol in my system! Was I going to be fun? Were people going to like me? Were my kids going to like me?'

Geoff and their children met her at the airport. Juli was a sweaty mess when the plane landed, 'But when I saw those three sweet faces I wanted to break down into a million pieces.'

It took all of her strength to get through those first few days back at the home that had once been awash with alcohol. There was a lot of positive self-talk. 'Find a way, Jules' became a mantra.

On the plus side, sobriety had a mesmerising freshness to it. 'Cooking, hanging out, watching TV – everything was different because I wasn't drunk,' Juli says. Clarity after so long in a fog was, in its own way, intoxicating. Addicts call these heady early days of success 'the pink cloud'. It's a honeymoon phase when things go well, a veil lifts and they feel confident and excited about their recovery, almost to the point of euphoria. Juli felt like she'd gained a super-power. 'I was like, "I'm a queen! I gave up alcohol!"' she says, punching the air. '"I'm gonna be sober forever! I can do this! This is a piece of cake!" Honestly, you feel so proud of yourself.'

The danger here is that hubris can create unrealistic expectations about the path to recovery and make an addict believe sobriety is easy – a mindset that can lead to relapse. As Juli's pink cloud started to fade and dark ones rolled in, she faced a daily fight with the part of her that wanted to take the easy path. 'Sometimes I feel like I'm two people,' she admits, 'because I'm always going back and forth in my own head. One voice is saying, "You're beautiful and strong and courageous." And the other one is saying, "But the taste of vodka would be so good."'

Some days it took all of Juli's will not to pick up a bottle. She recognised she had to go easy on herself, to keep calm and avoid the triggers that would ignite the desire to drink. 'You get grace from the people in your life and you also give yourself grace because you know that if this is going to work you have to actually start putting yourself first,' she says.

'My only job in those early days was to not drink. I had to sit in my shit, as I like to say. I had to learn how to navigate the feelings, how to handle the triggers, how to use my tools that my therapist had given me. I had to let go of all the little daily things that happen because I had to put all my energy into not taking a drink.'

Juli also had to find a way to manage the abundance of time that had landed in her lap now that she wasn't passing the hours in a drunken blur. On the good days she took to cleaning – purging unneeded possessions and organising the house. She went to the nursery and bought plants and pots and created a garden. But on the tougher days all she could manage was the school run before collapsing back into bed, exhausted from trying to be mentally strong.

She took baths, sometimes several times a day, because they allowed her to just sit and relax. As Juli steadied herself away from alcohol, she developed some new crutches – an addiction to peanut M&M's and cigarettes, which she still smokes. She tells me she's not proud of it and knows these vices are harmful too but, hey, first things first. 'You've given up a pretty big addiction so let's get that one done, then we'll get to this next part,' she reasons.

Juli orders more takeaway than she'd like, too, but mostly because cooking is still a trigger for her. For years every meal she cooked was prepared with a gathering unsteadiness and a bottle by her side.

Alcoholics and drug users often compare addiction to having a job, an all-consuming focus of each day. Juli felt the same about sobriety: *not* drinking became the main task of her waking hours. 'I'd wake up every morning and say, "Today you just don't have to drink." And then that would be my motto,' she recalls. 'And then I would go, "Okay, today you don't drink but you also have to tackle the laundry." I just had to learn grace.'

It's an ongoing lesson. Two years after Juli's last drink the family moved to Australia. It had always been part of the Ogilvys' long-term plans, and now with three teenagers, and alarmed by rising gun violence in the US, they decided it was time. Settling in Melbourne in 2019, close to Geoff's family, brought with it a raft of new emotional challenges, from loneliness to homesickness. Juli fell into depression: her marriage was hanging by a thread, and she struggled with the distance from her support network of family and friends in the States. I ask her if she was ever tempted to pick up the bottle during that time. 'Only once,' she says. After a fight with Geoff one night she grabbed the car keys and was ready to drive to the nearest bar and drown herself in vodka. Taking a moment of grace, she instead phoned her therapist in America.

Soon afterwards Juli deleted every drunk photo from her phone. 'I didn't ever want to see myself that ugly again,' she says. Her therapist, however, forced her to confront unsightly episodes from the past and question what role they played in her destructive relationship with alcohol. It was a painful and protracted journey of rediscovery. 'All you've done for years is pour bottle after bottle after bottle on top of it,' she says. 'It's so deep down there and when it comes out, it's hard.'

Over a couple of intense years, therapy peeled back the layers to finally address Juli's horrible teenage period. 'I had so much abandonment from my dad dying, which wasn't his fault, but I felt so much rejection that I looked for attention from a man,' Juli reasons. 'And then the rape – I'd just suppressed it. You get judged when you cry rape. You don't feel like anyone believes you. By getting sober, I had to talk about it.'

Telling the story from start to finish to her therapist and then again to me has lifted some of that weight from Juli. 'It's been therapeutic for me. I just needed someone to listen and to know that they believed me,' she says with a warm smile.

'It's also been very hard in the sense that it makes me so sad for who I was. She was so alone. And I'm anxious about everyone reading this. I'm proud but know that I will be judged as well, but I have to let go of that.'

'Have you ever contemplated taking action over the rape?' I ask.

'I've thought about confronting him,' she says slowly. 'I've written the letter a million times in my head, a million different versions. I'll never forget, but I've let go as much as I can. I've let go of the hatred for him, it doesn't serve me. That's on him. Karma is a beautiful thing and I trust in it even if I never see it play out.'

In acknowledging her emotional wounds and learning to treat them through therapy, Juli discovered a lot about herself. 'For one thing, that it's okay to feel uncomfortable,' she says evenly. It has also made her braver. 'I was so scared to be who I truly was,' she admits. Finding her courage changed Juli profoundly and that personal recalibration came at a cost. 'I used to be so scared to tell my husband I wasn't happy in our relationship.

'I didn't want to face what I knew was coming . . . all the changes I had to make and all the tough conversations that I needed to have. I don't think he understood how much it would change me and us.'

In finding herself, Juli lost her marriage.

'I just decided that who I was was actually pretty cool, and that it's okay to not give a shit what anyone else thinks,' she muses. 'I just want to live this beautiful, happy life where I'm loved and I love. I've had a big life; I've done special, fancy things, and that's all great, but I don't need that. I'm comfortable in my own skin. I love who I am and I know that my heart is the best thing about me.'

This isn't to say that Juli hasn't had some extremely challenging days, with her divorce, COVID lockdowns and distance from US family and friends over the past couple of years.

Juli and Geoff both live in Melbourne, and co-parent their three kids – week on, week off. 'It's the best for our kids. I wanted them to have time to settle in each week versus packing up a bag every couple of days. I miss them but use the time to recharge and get things done.'

Australia is now home for Juli. And finally, when the international borders reopened, her mum was on one of the first flights in from the US. In her sunny Melbourne home, Juli plays her favourite music and dances around the kitchen, feeling beautiful. She's a world away from those seedy sunrises when she had to face life at her drunken worst. 'I'd wake up in a shame spiral,' she says. 'The way I talked to myself every morning . . . there's no one in the world who could treat me like shit the way I did.'

Juli wants her story to serve as an important lesson for all women who face crises in their lives. 'Just to know that they are enough,' she says. 'Just how you are right now, everything about you is enough. And if someone doesn't like that, that's on them and not on you.'

She quotes a line from *The Wizard of Oz*, when Glinda the Good Witch says to Dorothy:

'You've always had the power, my dear. You just had to learn it for yourself.'

'I had the power for my own happiness the whole time,' Juli declares. 'You need to have that relationship with yourself first before you can give that to somebody else.'

Nowadays she focuses all that positive energy on her children. They watch TV shows that make them laugh, they play music and they laugh at Juli's dance moves. 'It brings me to my knees, the things that could have happened when I was drunk,' she says. 'And it's a daily practice to let that go.'

She's also making up for lost time. 'I think the biggest disservice I did to my kids while I was drinking was not taking them places,' she says. 'We stayed at home because I didn't want to get in the car and drive drunk.'

As ever, Juli draws strength from her support crew – the friends scattered around the world who she can call at any hour when she needs them. She leans on her mum and sister for comfort and says they're her biggest cheerleaders. And she mentions she wouldn't have made it through her divorce if not for the love and support of the girlfriends she's made in Melbourne. Juli did lose a few friends on the long road to recovery: the girls she used to party with who became uncomfortable around her and felt judged by her sobriety, as well as those who fell away due to the divorce. She only wishes the very best for them.

Every time we've sat down to chat over Zoom, Juli has been smothered by her three dogs, who fight for her attention. 'Can you say hi to Mel?' she says as a gorgeous honey-coloured labradoodle peers out of my monitor, big floppy ears, a lolling tongue and a smile. 'This is Jack,' she gushes. 'He's my soulmate right here.' Juli takes great comfort in their company, particularly when the kids are staying with their dad. 'I talk to the dogs like they're human and maybe it keeps me from going insane!' She laughs.

'A lot of people are frightened and struggling with the way the world is at the moment, so what's your best advice?' I ask.

Juli considers her answer for a few long beats before landing on one word: 'Perspective.'

'My therapist, Marcy, said to me, "I really want you to start thinking about perspective," and something just switched on,' Juli says. 'I realised I've been living my life in a funk, waiting for the good to come. Instead I need to realise how good life is and that when the bad comes you're going to get through it. The good will come again. So instead of letting anxiety take over, I try to talk kindly to myself, to tell myself it's all going to work out and it does. It's such a beautiful way to live, and it's so freeing.'

I tell her how happy I am that she saved herself, and how proud of her I am.

'I did it for no one but myself, Mel,' she replies. 'I love my children and I loved my husband, but I didn't even do it for them. I had to do it for me. I had to be my own hero in this story.'

Four

Aurelio

Most of us, to some degree, self-identify through the work we do. While I'm many things – a mum, a wife, a daughter, a fanatical GWS Giants supporter, a chatterbox and a '70s music tragic – in the past if ever I was asked I'd usually describe myself as a journalist. To be more precise, I saw myself as a *Channel 7* journalist.

The feminist in me used to say, 'My job doesn't define me!' But it really did, far more than I ever realised. Having left 7 after twenty-five years, it took a while for me to shake off the mindset that I was part of the network, and that it was somehow part of me. It was months before my phone got out of the habit of telling me it was 'twenty-five minutes to Martin Place, traffic is light'. It took time, too, for viewers to brush aside the illusion my profession had cast, and to see me for who I am. Not as the *Sunrise* woman, not as one half of 'Mel and Kochie', not as a newsreader, the *Sunday Night* anchor or a talking head, but as Melissa – your regular, flawed human being.

This change in my life coincided with the arrival of COVID and I empathised when it wrought devastation on millions of workers throughout the land. We all know someone who was badly affected as battered businesses reduced hours, cut back on staff or shut the doors entirely. I have felt for the young, in particular – the countless careers that were about to take off only to be grounded by lockdowns.

I thought a lot, too, about the people I've been privileged to meet who make their living in the arts: musicians, actors, directors and all those who beaver away behind the scenes in live entertainment who had their ambitions frozen in time. Many of these Australians, and countless others, struggled to support themselves during the pandemic, subsisting on the hope things would one day again be normal.

When the nation's mental health started to crumble alongside job losses and vanishing dreams, I spent a lot of time reflecting on a man I know who has endured much of this pain before.

Had you asked Aurelio Costarella to define himself, for thirty-four years he probably would have told you, humbly, that he was a dressmaker. He'd have been selling himself short. Cataloguing Aurelio's career highlights is like flipping through the glossiest pages of *Vogue*. There's Crown Princess Mary, barefoot on the floor of a Copenhagen palace, radiant and beautiful in layers of sepia and ivory silk tulle as sequins, hand-folded by Aurelio into tiny flowers, cascade from her shoulder into the folds of her gown. There's Charlize Theron, reclining on a table in a silk satin 1940s-inspired bias-cut dress, looking every inch the movie siren. Next up, Grammy-winning artist Rihanna rocking one of his beaded cocktail frocks on the red carpet in LA. And Aurelio will never forget the time Cate Blanchett appeared backstage at his show during Sydney Fashion Week to tell him it was her absolute favourite.

I first met Aurelio in the early 2000s, when I was lucky enough to wear his gowns to public events and his sharp tailoring on television. He truly has a way of making a woman feel her most beautiful, crafting a sexy leather skirt with as much flair as he drapes the most delicate of dresses.

My cherished pieces are now carefully stored and waiting to be passed on to my daughter. Far more valuable to me than the dresses, though, is the friendship I have forged with Aurelio.

He is a warm, gentle man who makes everyone feel like the star of his show. He is softly spoken, immaculately dressed – usually in black – handsome and stylish, as you'd expect from a designer. He's thoughtful, intelligent and brimming with wisdom. Behind the smile and the cloak of affability, however, Aurelio, like Juli, spent years shouldering an extremely painful emotional load in total secrecy. Away from the camera flashes, the glitz, the models and the blaze of publicity that comes with being an internationally acclaimed fashion designer, Aurelio would crumble into a sobbing heap in private. Often for days on end. Sometimes for weeks.

Although he was destined to rub shoulders with movie stars and rock royalty, the first muse to make Aurelio's heart sing could always be found in the corner of his family's lounge room in Perth on a Sunday afternoon. It was then, aged ten, that Aurelio would sit alongside his mum, Teresa, and watch *Young Talent Time*. Like Teresa, Aurelio adored Tina Arena, the seven-year-old daughter of Sicilian immigrants with the powerhouse voice. Watching her perform on TV each week was a cherished childhood ritual and, decades later, when he was invited to dress her for an Australian tour, Aurelio was immediately transported to the sofa of his childhood. 'I was like, "Oh my god! Oh my god! My mother is just going to be so excited about this!"'

Since Western Australia's borders were hermetically sealed during the pandemic, I was unable to interview Aurelio face-to-face, so we agreed to catch up for regular chats over Zoom during 2020 and 2021. It was a slow process as his story spans decades, and is as long as it is painful and, ultimately, inspiring.

Aurelio's parents, Pasquale and Teresa, hail from Reggio Calabria, on the coast of southern Italy. Pasquale made the voyage to Australia in 1956, leaving his pregnant wife and five-year-old daughter, Grazia, in Italy while he established himself in Perth.

Arriving with a suitcase and the equivalent of twenty dollars, Pasquale was determined to make a better life for his family in Australia. He started out picking potatoes for a pittance and later sought contracts for land clearing, gathering groups of men to spend weeks under the southern sun turning harsh bushland into paddocks. 'It was *hard* work,' Aurelio tells me, clearly proud of his father's grit.

After four years of sweat and toil, Pasquale was ready for his family to join him in Australia: Teresa, Grazia, who was now nine, and four-year-old Antonio, the son he hadn't yet met. They moved into a house in Northbridge shared with two other families they had travelled to Australia with, where, in lieu of rent, Teresa worked as a housekeeper, cook and cleaner.

By 1963 the Costarellas could afford their own home in North Perth, close to the city in a neighbourhood rich with Italian, Greek and Jewish culture. It was a time of great promise in Australia: Perth had just hosted the Commonwealth Games and the economy was revving on the back of a resources boom. Aurelio was born the following year – right into the lap of the Lucky Country.

The Costarellas were proud of their heritage. They spoke Italian at home, grew their own produce, and bottled wine and passata. These were the ingredients of a happy life, and the source of Pasquale's real passion. After years of backbreaking manual work, he bought a fruit and vegetable store in Mount Lawley, just a few minutes from home. Grazia, Antonio and Aurelio would head there after school to help out while Teresa prepared dinner in a kitchen out the back.

When she wasn't in the store, Teresa was at home, ensuring the house was spotless and her children were impeccably dressed. She designed and sewed all their clothes herself: beautiful dresses for Grazia, and shirts and pants for the boys. Aurelio became mesmerised by the process and watched in awe as his mum cut the lengths of fabric, and pinned and fitted her creations. To him it was some kind of alchemy. 'She never used patterns!' he exclaims. 'She would literally just lay out the cloth and chalk out the garment straight onto the cloth and cut. And I just thought, "Wow!"'

Like the master's apprentice, Aurelio watched Teresa guide the fabric between her fingers, listening to the rhythmic hum as she fed it into the hungry teeth of her treasured Singer treadle sewing machine – one of the few things she was able to bring from the old country.

Aurelio recounts how his mother told him the story of the Singer not long before she passed away in 2017.

'Her mother had wanted her to have a trade,' he explains. 'So she sent my mum to sewing classes – to the maestra, the local dressmaker – and as it turns out Mum was an amazing dressmaker.' Times were tough in post-war Italy, however, and Teresa's father forbade her mother from buying her a sewing machine.

'But my grandmother was determined,' Aurelio says with a warm smile. 'She saved and scrimped and so did my dad, and between the two of them they got enough money to buy Mum a second-hand Singer treadle.'

The young Teresa could never have imagined the elegant-looking contraption would travel halfway around the world with her. Nor could she have dreamed the machine – bought for her with so much love – would one day ignite the career of one of Australia's most talented designers, her cherished youngest son. Today Teresa's timeworn Singer resides in the Western Australian Museum, alongside one of Aurelio's gowns.

'What was she like?' I ask one day.

It's a wide question and, of course, the answer is complicated. Aurelio describes his mother as 'caring and tender, strict when she needed to be'. But he also remembers the many days when she wouldn't – or couldn't – get out of bed. He knew she wasn't well, but he had no idea what, specifically, she was dealing with.

It wasn't until later in life that Aurelio learned she was admitted to hospital a few months after he was born with what he now suspects was postnatal depression. With Pasquale away working for weeks at a time, it fell to thirteen-year-old Grazia to look after Aurelio while their mother underwent electroconvulsive therapy. Better known as 'shock therapy', it was developed in Italy in the 1930s and works by using electricity to induce seizures. For many it conjures horrible scenes from the movie *One Flew Over the Cuckoo's Nest*. But it proved successful in many people and is still used today to treat patients with severe depression or bipolar disorder who haven't responded to other treatments.

Aurelio says his family tended to sweep his mother's condition under the carpet. 'Mum would always refer to it as her "nerves",' he says. 'It was a "nervous disorder", which was anxiety, but there was very little understanding of what that was.' Such things were never discussed.

Today, through the eyes of a grown man, Aurelio sees that even as a small boy he was beginning to show symptoms similar to his mother's. But at the time, no one noticed. 'The fact that I was a very anxious child was not something that anyone ever picked up on, and I didn't have the under-standing to know that I felt differently to anybody else,' he explains. 'I knew that there were things that obviously terrified me and I had a lot of irrational fear, but I can only recognise that now as an adult.'

Aurelio was a painfully shy boy and disliked school. He dreaded the bus ride and was too terrified to speak in class. At home, when other kids played outside, he chose to stay indoors painting, cooking or watching his mother sew. Even in his teenage years he was far happier staying at home and studying. A good student who was naturally creative, he was accepted into Curtin University to study architecture.

During his second year at uni, however, Aurelio realised his passion lay in the design and construction of clothes, not buildings. 'A group of friends and I decided that as a bit of a joke we would do a home economics class that was basically dressmaking, learning to sew from Simplicity Patterns,' he recalls. 'It was very basic, just to break the monotony of architectural studies.'

It may have been a frivolous flirtation for his friends, but as soon as Aurelio began, he felt possibilities woven into the fabric and quickly became hooked. 'I started getting really creative with the patterns,' he enthuses. 'I was inspired by Vivienne Westwood's Worlds End label and it was when Japanese designers were first making huge inroads into Paris, Comme des Garçons and Yamamoto, and I just loved what they were doing.'

He commandeered the dining-room table at home, along with his mum's trusty Singer, and started making dresses and tunics with long, full dirndl skirts with petticoat layers. 'Post-Apocalyptic Buffalo Girl' is how he describes it now. Aurelio even had Teresa help out. 'She was on the machine and I was tie-dyeing and shredding calico, cheesecloth . . . it was all very deconstructed back then,' he says. 'It was a period in fashion that was not about glamour.'

The next step was to try to sell the pieces he'd produced. Using the anglicised version of his name, given to him on his first day of school by a teacher who found 'Aurelio' too hard to master, the fashion label Ray Costarella was born.

In 1983, at the age of nineteen, Aurelio began selling through a local boutique in Perth called Creme Soda, owned by his soon-to-be business partner, Kerry Giles. He worked in the store during the day and made clothes at night. It was such a success that by the end of the first year, 70 per cent of the store's sales were his designs. 'And before I knew it I made the decision that this is what I wanted to do,' he says.

Aurelio bit the bullet and dropped out of university in his second year. 'And of course my parents were mortified,' he says, with a dramatic roll of his eyes. They begged him to get a 'normal job' like his brother Antonio, an electrical engineer with Telecom. 'But that's not me,' Aurelio pleaded with them. 'I don't want a normal job!'

Their persistent objections only fuelled his ambition. 'That actually drove me to want to prove to them that I could do this,' Aurelio says. Rather than being a waste of time, his two years at university proved invaluable. 'I taught myself to make patterns based on what I'd learned studying architecture,' he says. 'I would visualise a garment laid out flat, as a plan, always very three-dimensional and sculptural, and I would drape a lot of pieces directly onto a form. I had this ability to visualise a garment and then imagine that laid out flat.'

Soon he was selling enough pieces that he could afford to take a share in the boutique. Two years later he bought it outright – the first of many retail outlets he'd open in Perth. Aurelio became a big fish in a comparatively small pond, and he knew he wanted more. In 1989, with one massive suitcase packed with his precious collection, he flew to Sydney. 'I didn't know anyone in the industry,' he remembers. 'I just landed, unpacked the collection in my room at the Hilton Hotel and started cold-calling people.'

By now his designs were much more refined. 'Structured cocktail dresses in silk taffeta featuring mini pannier skirts with sculptural silk rosettes on the hips, boned corsets covered in heavy white guipure lace and silk ottoman belle skirts . . .'

'Ooh-la-la!' I exclaim.

Aurelio chuckles knowingly but says the gamble to back himself paid off. By the end of his first day in Sydney, he'd landed an agent and his first account. 'There were stores in Sydney called Suyu,' he recalls. 'I got my first order from them – $25,000, which back then was a lot of money – and I thought, "Oh my god, this is actually happening!"'

A few days later Aurelio took his suitcase to Melbourne and repeated the process, calling complete strangers out of the blue. 'And that,' he says, clapping his hands together, 'was the beginning.'

Before long Ray Costarella had accounts across Australia, and an investor to help the label expand. He opened high-end stores in Claremont in Perth and the ritzy Strand Arcade in Sydney. Hard work and following his heart had paid off, just as it had for his father. His parents were still not overly impressed with his career choice but he used that as fuel for his fire. 'They were really tough,' Aurelio tells me. 'I had to work really hard to crack them, but it just made me more determined.'

In 1996, just a few years later, however, the partnership with his investor flamed out and Aurelio came crashing back to earth. It was messy and in the end he had to walk away from the wreckage of the brand and declare himself bankrupt.

The apparent end of his dream brought Aurelio to the brink, financially and emotionally. Suffocating beneath the rubble of his perceived failure, he experienced his first 'breakdown'. 'I just spiralled into this very deep, dark depression,' he says quietly.

By then Aurelio was living in Perth, and there was a particularly bad period when he barely left the house for three months. 'If someone knocked on the door, I would hide,' he says. 'If the phone rang, I wouldn't answer it. I was just so terrified of having any sort of interaction. I lived in a perpetual state of fear.'

Aurelio knew he needed help and eventually saw a doctor who diagnosed him with clinical depression and prescribed antidepressants. Acknowledging he was mentally unwell was a difficult and daunting process given his childhood experience of watching his mother struggle with her own mental health. Aurelio told no one of his diagnosis and held on to an unfilled script for months. Only when his depression worsened and the darkness became intolerable did he finally accept that medication appeared to be his only option. 'I resisted because I had several friends who had been on medication and ended up in psych wards,' he recalls. 'I'd seen how it had affected them, but it got to the point where I was in such a bad place I had to do something.'

Aurelio walked into a chemist in Perth, had the script filled and walked back outside into a living hell.

Clinical depression, also known as major depressive disorder, describes when a patient has persistent feelings of intense sadness that affect their mental and physical health. It typically interferes with the person's daily life. In other words, it is debilitating. According to the Black Dog Institute, one in seven Australians will experience depression in their lifetime. Aurelio was one of them.

Globally speaking, Australia has some unenviable statistics when it comes to mental health. It's estimated that as many as one in six Australians are living with anxiety, and that one in sixteen have depression, while three million are reliant on antidepressants. An OECD report from 2015 found that Australians were the second-highest users of antidepressants in the world behind Iceland, where the world is in frozen darkness for half the year.

Aurelio says there was no comfort in knowing he wasn't alone. Unwell, exhausted, defeated, bankrupt and concealing all this from family and friends, he was convinced the magical future he had imagined for himself was gone forever. This was the first time Aurelio experienced suicidal thoughts. 'I felt I had failed myself and everyone around me. I didn't want any part of life and certainly had no desire to step back into the fashion industry, it was all just too hard,' he admits. A quieter lifestyle seemed to beckon. 'I actually wanted to move down south and grow herbs,' he says.

And still he kept his condition secret, even from his family. 'I spent years hiding the fact I was on antidepressants,' Aurelio says with sadness. 'Even though my mother had a history of mental ill health, I didn't want her to worry about me because she was the eternal worrier, and it was just easier to not talk about it with anyone. The sense of fear and shame and failure was too great.'

Aurelio was plotting his sea change and making inquiries about studying naturopathy when he received an unexpected call from a retailer in Adelaide. It was an invitation to launch a label for them. Crucially, the offer gave Aurelio the chance to be creative without the burden of running a business – a gentle, low-pressure way to get back to doing what he loved most.

'I thought, "This sounds okay because it's not mine, but I do have creative control,"' he explains.

Aurelio signed on and the MILK label was born. It showed at Fashion Week in Sydney in 1998. The first store to see and buy the collection was the legendary luxury outlet Barneys New York. 'It was quite a coup!' says Aurelio. So much so it reignited his burning passion for design and lifted his confidence. He designed for MILK for about eighteen months. 'It was enough time to get back on my feet.'

Ditching 'Ray' and reclaiming his identity and place in the industry with his birthname Aurelio Costarella, his new namesake brand was unveiled at Fashion Week in Sydney in 2000. He'd called the collection FREEFALL. 'I was thirty-five, had no money, financed the collection and the show with a credit card, and was terrified on show day, hence the name of the collection,' he says. 'It was a huge leap of faith, this was make or break. The show had just finished and I was emotionally exhausted, and I burst into tears when Karin Upton Baker, then editor-in-chief at *Harper's Bazaar*, tapped me on the shoulder and said,

"We loved the show and I have someone here who wants to meet you." I looked over her shoulder to see Cate Blanchett, guest editor for the magazine, and just stood clutching Cate's hand and sobbing. A moment I'll never forget.'

His designs were instantly in hot demand around the world, sought after by Hollywood actresses and prestigious department stores. He even sparked a bidding war in Australia between David Jones and Myer. The pinnacle, however, was his first show at New York Fashion Week in February 2007 and Paris Fashion Week in 2013, followed by his induction into the Design Institute of Australia's Hall of Fame in 2016.

Aurelio's gowns have since been displayed in the Western Australian Museum in *Aurelio Costarella: A 30 Year Retrospective*, the National Gallery of Victoria and the Powerhouse Museum in Sydney. He has been feted for his artistry and audacious, exquisite detailing. Imagine ostrich feathers, velvet and crystals, sculptural corsetry and romantic, luxurious glamour.

He also carefully crafted a sublime mask of confidence and contentedness to wear in public. In private, though, he was starting to fall apart at the seams. 'I was pretending I was okay,' Aurelio says. He was experiencing more success than he ever dreamed possible, but that only brought immense pressure and stress, not relief. Greater highs meant deeper lows and, now that he had more to lose, Aurelio was gripped by fear.

I tell him how stunned I am to learn he'd been going through this at the time we were getting to know each other. 'You always struck me as being so at home in the fashion industry,' I say. 'It seemed to me like you were in your element.'

Aurelio laughs darkly at my assessment. 'There were moments in the lead-up to a show at Fashion Week where I would literally be in bed, just hiding out of fear,' he confides. 'My mind would be racing, going: "Oh my god! What if it's not good enough? What if they don't like the collection?" Having to put yourself on the line every season was probably one of the hardest things, because with each collection I was being judged on how good it was, or did retailers like it?'

When he explains it like that, I can imagine the pressure would have been almost unbearable, even without fighting against depression. In the world of fashion, one collection can make or break a designer. It's like living with a jewel-encrusted guillotine over your neck.

By 2010 Aurelio had a staff of fourteen and retail stores and was travelling for six months of the year. Once again, the weight of managing the business side of his career began to damage the artistic side. 'It all came down to opinions and numbers and dollars, and having to keep the business model viable and my employees paid,' he says. 'It was not just about me and my creative process, it was so much bigger than me, and I took all of that on with every collection. Immense anxiety and fear.'

We're all familiar with fear, even terror. My experiences of being terrified range from the shock of a car bomb detonating near where I was staying in Beirut, to waiting side-of-stage to host an event in the Great Hall of Parliament House, my heart pounding so hard I worried it would crack a rib.

Fear is a strange emotion. It can be triggered by something real or imagined. It can render us frozen, but it can also mobilise us: the flight-or-fight response.

I ask Aurelio how he managed to keep going during that period of fear. He shrugs and says he simply chose to fight. 'I don't think I'd yet heard the expression "Feel the fear and do it anyway", but in retrospect that's what I was doing for so many years,' he says. 'I was feeling that fear, it was tangible, but my desire to succeed – coupled with my need to please my parents – was greater, and that was the difference for me.'

He may have stiffened his upper lip but that didn't stop the panic attacks.

'Can you describe what a panic attack feels like?' I probe gently.

He takes a deep breath and looks me in the eye from 2000 kilometres away. 'It's literally just this snap of feeling that you can't breathe and your heart just starts racing, and it's heavy and you're flushed and sweating,' he begins. 'There are moments when you feel like you're just going to die because you can't take that next breath. You're gasping for air.'

The symptoms can be terrifying, and for Aurelio it's still very raw. 'As I'm telling you this I'm actually feeling it,' he adds. Naturally I suggest we change the subject but Aurelio insists we push on. It's important, he says, that people understand what a panic attack is. 'No, I'm not having an anxiety attack right now,' he reassures me, 'but whenever I think about them it takes me back to that moment. Your stomach starts to tighten up. It can last for a minute or two or it can be longer. And sometimes I would just start sobbing, feeling that I had no control over what was happening. I now know that you do, you actually have to breathe. You actually need to pause at that moment and breathe deeply.'

The Australian Bureau of Statistics estimates that anxiety disorders affect around 17 per cent of Australians, and Beyond Blue says up to 40 per cent of us will experience a panic attack at some point in our life.

These usually last from several minutes to around half an hour. The symptoms can feel very similar to those of a heart attack. Untreated, they can be severely disabling and disruptive as sufferers are reluctant to do things or go to places that might trigger one. It was this kind of invisible cage that Aurelio found himself a prisoner in.

In January 2015 he was showing a collection in Sydney when a major panic attack sent him spiralling out of control. 'I read a work email and I just snapped!' he says. 'I was sobbing. I couldn't stop crying. I was on the bathroom floor in my hotel room just literally in a foetal position sobbing.' He tells me this was the moment he finally admitted to himself that he desperately needed serious help. 'I didn't have any other options if I wanted to survive,' he says.

A few days later Aurelio admitted himself to a private clinic in Perth. 'I sent my GP a text message saying, "Five years ago when you told me that I needed to take some time out, and perhaps take care of myself, and I told you I didn't have time, you were right. I'm in the clinic." She'd tried to warn me a few times that this is what I needed to do, but I couldn't see it then.'

Business had got in the way, and so had pride. 'It was something that I'd resisted for the longest time,' Aurelio admits. 'I was terrified of what people would think, terrified of it leaking to the media, terrified of being judged. But I soon came to the realisation that this wasn't about anybody else. Ultimately, this was about me and my own wellbeing.'

Life inside a mental health clinic was a confronting change of pace for the former high-flyer. 'What am I doing here?' he remembers thinking. 'I didn't think I would last more than a few days.' Soon enough, an unexpected encounter realised his worst fears. 'It was my first day, I went to the dining room and I was waiting to get some food when this young woman walked straight up to me and she said, "You're Aurelio Costarella! What are you doing here?"'

It was one of his former models. The terror that his mental condition would now be made public added 'a whole other level of fear and anxiety for me'.

So began three years of treatment, initially as an inpatient. Looking back now, Aurelio says much of this time in and around the clinic was a blur of medication, therapy, confusion and frustration. He was already taking sleep medication but his psychiatrist prescribed even more. 'There would be one med and then there were two meds and then before I knew it there were three meds,' Aurelio says with a disbelieving shake of the head.

And that was just the sleeping pills. The increasing daily allocation of medication seemed relentless. 'Two weeks later, I'd gone from being on a low dose of an antidepressant and one benzodiazepine for my anxiety to being on eight different medications: three antidepressants, two off-label antipsychotics, two benzodiazepines, and thyroxine, and this combination triggered serotonin syndrome.'

Many medications used to treat depression affect serotonin levels in the brain. Being on multiple similar medications can lead to serotonin syndrome, which brings with it symptoms such as elevated heart rate, headaches, confusion and agitation – precisely what Aurelio was feeling.

He figured he had no choice but to cling for dear life to the chemical roller-coaster: amphetamines on the way up and tranquillisers on the way down, each drug stretching him from one extreme to the other as they worked to counterbalance. He was irritable and anxious, and 'felt like death' for days on end.

During this period he became inadvertently dependent on benzodiazepines, or benzos, as they're colloquially known. After a while, Aurelio couldn't function without them. When I ask why he didn't query this diet of drugs at the time, he replies that he had faith in the system helping him, and he never questioned the directions of his psychiatrist. Instead of helping him recover, Aurelio says the treatment almost destroyed him.

Managing his mental health required every minute of Aurelio's time and every last fibre of his will. Running a fashion empire was simply out of the question, and in 2017 he announced on social media he was closing the label to seek treatment for his mental health. Like everyone who knows him, I was taken aback by the news. I reached out to Aurelio, sent him my love and offered my support in any way I could, but I had no idea how dire my poor friend's life had become, or how long he'd been struggling alone.

In walking away from his business, Aurelio felt like he'd left himself in the past, and now faced an uncertain future like a ghost. After thirty-four years as a fashion designer, it had become his identity. 'Leading up to closing my business, I'd already started grieving,' he says. 'I was grieving for the fact that I wasn't able to carry on. It was a loss of identity, that whole idea of, "What am I going to do from here? This is who I've been for all of these years! Who am I without the brand?"'

After three years of treatment, including fifty-one weeks as an inpatient, Aurelio was discharged and sent home. He wasn't getting any better. He was simply adrift on a roiling sea of emotions and drugs, and something needed to change. 'I just couldn't do it anymore,' he says.

A lot had happened in that time. His beloved mum, Teresa, had passed away at the age of eighty-five, and Aurelio had split from his long-term partner. Now, he was alone in his Mount Lawley home in inner-city Perth, and his life was almost unrecognisable from the one he'd known.

It was in this strange new world of limbo that Aurelio noticed something even more sinister was happening to him. He started having suicidal thoughts and suffered dreadful, violent nightmares about murdering his friends. 'I had this cascade of symptoms that included paranoia, nightmares and depersonalisation,' he says. 'I felt like I wasn't in my body and had little control over my thoughts, and I didn't understand what was happening.'

It turned out he was experiencing benzodiazepine withdrawal.

Benzodiazepines, including Valium, are a class of psychoactive drugs that work as minor tranquillisers, slowing messages between the brain and body, and affecting physical, mental and emotional responses. They are used to treat anxiety and are generally considered safe and effective for short-term use over two to four weeks. Anything longer can lead to dependency. Aurelio had been on high doses of benzodiazepines for more than 200 weeks – too long to simply go cold turkey. Instead, he had begun the process of reduction, but coming off benzodiazepines is not easy or quick. It's a slow process of tapering.

Benzo withdrawal can literally be a nightmare, more so the longer a patient has been on them. Symptoms range from disturbed sleep, headaches and panic attacks to hallucinations, psychosis and suicidal ideation.

Aurelio's mental health was clearly much worse than when he'd first been admitted to the clinic. He'd tried to do the right thing to help himself, but by the time he realised he was being harmed instead of helped it was too late. 'The suicidal thoughts were worse than when I was going through my darkest days with depression and anxiety,' he says.

There were weeks on end when Aurelio couldn't leave the house, and days when even the thought of getting out of bed was too overwhelming. He suffered memory loss, couldn't focus for more than half an hour and found driving too dangerous to contemplate. On top of all that he became hypersensitive to light and sound. 'Going to a supermarket for me was akin to walking into a nightclub,' he says. 'I would have to race in there, grab what I needed and get out of there as quickly as possible.'

I point out that Aurelio experienced lockdown and self-imposed social distancing long before COVID forced it on the rest of us. The realisation that treatment had left him in far worse shape than his original condition was also something that had parallels during the coronavirus pandemic. One of the biggest debates in the scientific community through 2020 and 2021 was around the notion that lockdowns might be more damaging to mental health than the risks posed by opening up.

As Aurelio came to understand his symptoms, he also recognised in himself similarities to his mother's anxiety. 'I remember saying to my sister, Grazia, "I get it! I understand how Mum had been feeling for the last ten, fifteen years of her life because that's how I'm feeling now!" Mum hated going out, she just couldn't deal with being around people, and that's exactly the person I became.'

At the time of her death, Teresa had been taking benzodiazepines for fifty-four years. She'd first been prescribed Valium when pregnant with Aurelio, but back in 1964 there was no awareness of the risks. It's now understood that benzodiazepines can pass through the placenta. 'So in all probability the indications are there that I would have had some level of benzo withdrawal as a child,' Aurelio points out.

At the time of writing he is *still* trying to taper off Valium, an agonisingly slow process. 'I've been tapering by 0.125 milligrams at a time, when I can tolerate it or I feel strong enough,' he says. 'It's taken me three years to reduce 10 milligrams of Valium.' In the clinic there were days when he was having the equivalent of 70 to 80 milligrams across diazepam, lorazepam and clonazepam.

Increasingly angry and frustrated at the treatment he had received, Aurelio lodged a complaint about negligent prescribing with the Australian Health Practitioner Regulation

Agency (AHPRA) and embarked on a legal campaign to access his records from the clinic. After a two-year fight he was finally given four large volumes containing thousands of pages of notes. The records showed Aurelio had been fed twenty-three different medications over those three years with no record of informed consent. 'Three of them were a cocktail of benzodiazepines taken concurrently. I was on a number of antipsychotics, lithium and two stimulants, all prescribed off-label,' he says. The AHPRA asked an independent psychiatrist to examine Aurelio's medical records but he didn't find any wrongdoing.

Thoroughly unimpressed, Aurelio consulted medical negligence lawyers but was advised that the cost and time involved – with no guarantee of success – made it a case not worth pursuing. Most people would have left the matter there, but Aurelio had an ace up his nicely tailored sleeve – he happened to be an internationally feted fashion designer and, as such, legal case or not, he had a platform.

Having spent years dreading the thought that his mental health struggles would end up fodder for the press, Aurelio became emboldened by the power of his celebrity. Nowadays, by speaking publicly about his ordeal, he's hoping to bring about changes in the mental health sector around informed consent, and raise awareness of the long-term effects and potential harm of psychoactive medication taken as prescribed. He also advocates for more community support away from the hospital system as a way of mitigating the need for crisis care.

Aurelio says his is a cautionary tale, and he believes sharing it will potentially save lives. 'Any advocacy work or campaigning that I do, I'm doing to stop other people going through what I've gone through,' he says. 'That is so important to me. This is about the system taking some accountability. I'm not anti-medication, but twenty-three drugs over three years didn't do me any good and in fact did me a great deal of harm. We need more information to understand the risks.'

My conversations with Aurelio were long and deeply personal. We only spoke on days when he felt strong enough, and at times it felt like I was hitching a short ride on his roller-coaster. One day I'd be applauding his strength and perseverance, the next I was wiping tears as he described his pain.

With the grinding gloom of a global pandemic in mind, I ask him how he gets through those 'other days', the really hard ones when the end isn't visible, the last steps of his recovery feel overwhelming and he wonders if he will ever get free of benzodiazepines. 'I find joy in small things and give gratitude for what I have,' he affirms. 'When I've been through the worst moments of suicidal ideation, I've been able to separate it out so that I understand that it's not me, it's actually the medication. I don't want to die. I have learned to find ways of focusing on the moment.'

'And when you can't reach that place?' I ask.

'Well, sometimes I just sit with the distress and the discomfort and really dig into it and ask, "Okay, what is this? What is it that I'm actually feeling?" Breaking it down into moments and days rather than focusing long term has helped me enormously.'

In 2019, while Aurelio was having a particularly awful withdrawal episode, his sister, Grazia, died suddenly, a painful and tragic reminder of life's fragility. 'It made me realise how much I have to live for,' he says. 'Her last words to me before she died were, "Are you okay?" It made me realise she would have wanted me to fight this, that there are things I have to do and things I need to do. So I'm not going anywhere.'

With so much to work through emotionally, this once lonely and secretive man now looks for hope and direction wherever he can. Lately he's found it in an online community of people struggling with prescribed harm. 'It's where I've found my strength,' he tells me. 'Early on I was helped by someone based in Texas. She's still supporting me, and now I'm doing the same to the people that I've been introduced to in Australia. So now I'm giving back. It's a cycle of the harmed helping the harmed.'

Aurelio hasn't designed a garment in more than six years. I ask him if he'd ever go back, and he says no, albeit slowly and with hesitation. But nowadays his creative outlet is art. He started painting as a form of therapy when he was in the clinic, and never stopped. He says it is a form of meditation. 'I don't have to deal with anyone,' he chuckles. 'I don't have to talk to anyone. I put some music on and I lose myself in my work.'

He always Zoomed in to my home office from his art room. Propped up behind him, giant half-painted canvases spoke of a swirl of emotions. 'Some days it's light and col-ourful and other days it's darker and moodier,' he points out, glancing over at the hues and shapes on the easels. 'I have maybe five or six pieces on the go at any given time and I go to whichever piece I'm drawn to on that particu-lar day. For the most part, creatives are innately sensitive beings, and mental health issues tend to come with that creativity.'

His abstract works are in high demand and Aurelio donates 10 per cent from each sale to Lifeline, and produces a separate piece annually to be auctioned. When I ask him how he'd describe himself today, Aurelio is happy to let his job define him. 'I call myself an artist now,' he says after a long pause. 'I had imposter syndrome for ages,' he says, 'but I actually feel comfortable now telling people that, yes, I'm an artist.'

Once again, he's selling himself short. He may be an artist, but Aurelio Costarella is so much more: he's an advocate, an inspiration, a gentleman, a survivor and a great teacher.

Five

Rachel

Although it was his choice, it broke my heart that Aurelio had initially suffered alone, hiding his pain from the world until he found the strength to speak out and advocate on behalf of other victims. Even as he clawed his way back towards the light in recent years, he generally resisted the interventions of others. The day he told me that any kind of group therapy was too much for him to bear – because it would only add other people's pain to his own – I desperately wished I could have given him a hug.

We are all wired differently but, for the most part, I've

tended to talk about my hurt and struggles with people close to me. I hold faith in the adage that a problem shared is a problem halved. This world view, of course, takes two at least. Aurelio's solitary stoicism caused me to think a lot about the worth of sharing another human being's pain, of choosing to walk with them through the fire. No one I know understands this more than Rachel Martin.

Rachel didn't feel a thing the moment her life changed forever on 23 August 2012. She was fast asleep in a back-packers' hostel in New Zealand while, on the other side of the world, the man she loved, Curtis McGrath, was flat on his back, dazed and confused as a shower of dirt and stones fell on him from a pale desert sky. Moments earlier the 6'4" Australian Army sapper had been patrolling a dusty track in a perilous corner of war-torn Afghanistan. He'd been sent into a Taliban-controlled province to sweep for IEDs. Curt's unit had already cleared four bombs that day and as Rachel dozed more than 13,000 kilometres away, the fifth detonated beneath his feet.

Military shorthand for 'improvised explosive device', IEDs were synonymous with the war in Afghanistan, and they haunted the dreams of all whose loved ones served there. Before Curt deployed, Rachel had watched a TV documentary about the devastating impact IEDs have on the human body. Later, as Curt was packing his bags for war, Rachel raised the elephant in the room: 'Have you thought about what you're going to do if you lose your legs?'

Rachel had learned a lot about the Taliban's cheap and very nasty homemade bombs. Some were enormous, capable of blowing armoured trucks into the air. Smaller devices targeted soldiers on foot. The IED that landed Curt on his back was about the size of a 600 ml soft-drink bottle. When he regained his senses in the falling debris that day, he tried to pull himself up into a half-sitting position using his elbows, and assess what had happened. Curt couldn't seem to balance, and that's when he saw both of his legs were gone – just as the enemy had intended.

A major study of IED casualties by Canadian trauma surgeons found that the crude bombs were more likely to cause amputations than the landmines used in World War II. The tactical aims of maiming rather than killing, however, remained the same: to put stress on an enemy's medical resources, to remove from the battlefield extra soldiers needed to care for the wounded, and to effect a sickening assault on morale.

What research is yet to measure, however, is the fallout IEDs have on people outside the theatre of war. The bomb that claimed Curt's legs triggered another kind of shockwave, one that engulfed the people who loved him. Phone call by terrible phone call, the horrifying news was passed along. It reached his most beloved – the beautiful, funny medical student he'd started dating a year earlier – around 6 am New Zealand time.

Rachel had dreams of how her life would unfurl. She and Curt were only twenty-four, young enough to feel invincible but mature enough to have well-considered plans. With her handsome, kind and loving man towering beside her, Rachel envisaged renovating an old house in New Zealand, having a few children and a dog. She'd work as a doctor; he'd join the New Zealand Police.

In a heartbeat, that imagined road ahead had been wiped off the map. Instead, Rachel suddenly found herself wrestling with terrible questions partners, family members and friends the world over have to face after fit young men are sent off to war only to return broken.

What should she do? What *could* she do? What was her role now that the person she loved had been cut down in this way? How could she stay strong for him? How could she help him find a new purpose and identity while maintaining her own? How much was she allowed to grieve for the life they'd dreamed up together, now seemingly gone forever? Was she allowed to feel like a casualty, too, when she was physically as fit as a fiddle?

'I'd gone from dating this person, thinking of this life we were going to have together and being able to see that, to potentially going to have a life with someone with no legs,' Rachel explains from her home on the Gold Coast.

Perhaps the biggest, scariest question was the one she'd sometimes circle back to when there were no clear answers to all the others. 'I definitely had moments where I thought, "Am I going to be able to do this at all? Is this something I'll be strong enough to do?"'

In other words, should she leave Curt and try to get on with her life without him? The answer was sometimes elusive, but along the way to finding it, Rachel learned more about herself — and about love and the bond of a problem shared — than many people do in a lifetime.

In 2017 my husband, John, held a fundraising lunch for Legacy, the charity that supports the families of killed and injured veterans. Curt was the guest speaker; it was the first time he'd told a room full of strangers what had happened to him in Afghanistan. I'd been asked to conduct what's known in the business as a 'fireside chat' with Curt; my questions gently led him through the horrors of his experience. It's supposed to be a little less confronting than having to stand at a lectern and deliver a speech on your own. I hope it was easier for Curt, because I found listening to his story firsthand incredibly difficult.

John continued to help Curt manage media and sponsorship arrangements, and I kept looking at him through the lens of a journalist, fascinated by his story and his capacity to pick himself up. When he'd come to Sydney, he'd stay at our place, and over many late nights and bottles of red wine I got to know the man behind the narrative. And then on one trip, he brought his fiancée, Rachel Martin, and I developed an instant, full-blown girl crush.

Rachel is a gorgeous red-headed New Zealand-born, English-raised doctor with a dark sense of humour she uses to break the ice when people don't know what to say. She once posted a photo to her Instagram account of Curt's prosthetic legs leaning against a wall, their dog 'asleep at his master's feet'. Getting to know her over the past five years has been one of my life's great pleasures.

Rachel was seventeen when her family moved from the UK to Dunedin in New Zealand's South Island in 2005. The change in hemisphere turned her life upside down in more ways than one. She'd been a popular straight-A student who dreamed of becoming a doctor, but in New Zealand she was saddled with the cruel nickname 'Foreigner' and struggled to make friends. Her grades plummeted, too.

Rachel's parents, Tony and Katherine, wouldn't let her outsource blame for poor schoolwork to the class bullies. 'Mum and Dad used to tell me it was my responsibility to make it work,' Rachel says as we chat over Zoom (the Queensland border had also been slammed shut). 'It was ultimately up to me how I wanted to approach my life and be in control of my happiness.'

Seizing on those words – which would return to her as a mantra in the years ahead – Rachel took a firm grip on her future. In 2006 she graduated from high school with enough marks to study microbiology and immunology at the University of Otago.

Meanwhile, across the Tasman Sea, in Australia, the ambitions of another young New Zealander were taking shape. Curt's family had moved to a farm in Western Australia when he was ten. He spent hours staring into the blue sky stretched across the wheatfields and dreaming of being a jet pilot. The McGraths moved back to Queenstown in New Zealand's South Island until Curt finished high school, then relocated to Brisbane. At eighteen he joined the Australian Army to train as a combat engineer.

Rachel was nineteen and in her first year of university in Dunedin when their worlds collided. A university pal of Rachel's named Tyson announced one day that a friend of his was coming to visit. Tyson called the mysterious stranger 'Hot Army Curt'. Rachel remembers scoffing: 'We'll see how hot this Hot Army Curt is!'

A few days later she walked straight into him in the hallway while visiting Tyson. Like in a scene from a rom-com, Rachel was frozen to the spot, face-to-face with Curt and completely lost for words. 'I said . . . *nothing*!' she laughs. 'I just *stared* at him!'

She did a quick U-turn and scurried back upstairs to the flat her girlfriends shared. 'He's *really* hot!' Rachel blurted as she burst through the door.

'They all said, "You're such a weirdo. Did you say hi?"' Rachel recalls. 'And I said, "No, I walked out! I was so embarrassed!"'

Although the moment was more Rachel from *Friends* than Rachel the focused microbiology student, she knew in those few seconds face-to-face with Curt that she'd one day marry him. He was totally different from the boys she knew – magnetically so. 'He was a breath of fresh air,' Rachel says. 'He had his life together. He was doing humanitarian work. He was great!'

It was another twelve months, however, before they'd meet again. Fresh from jungle training in Malaysia, Curt returned to New Zealand to visit his mates. This time Rachel was ready. 'I thought, "Game on! Curt's coming!

Brilliant!"' she recalls with a gleam in her eye. 'I bought a new dress. I was on a mission.'

That night, as the group hit student bars in downtown Dunedin, Rachel became Curt's shadow. 'I basically just stalked him,' she says, laughing. Curt noticed. 'He said, "Wherever I looked, you were right behind me, just staring at me,"' Rachel says. 'Finally he said to himself, "I've got to kiss her or she won't leave me alone."'

It was a brief moment at the bar and there was an instant connection, but Curt had to leave again ahead of a deployment to East Timor. They messaged each other intermittently via Facebook, more as friends than anything else, as Rachel continued her studies in New Zealand.

After completing her degree in 2010, Rachel moved to Canberra for a year to do a graduate diploma in science communication. When that was done she took a summer-holiday job on Fraser Island. When deadly floods devastated much of South East Queensland, Rachel found herself out of work, alone and unable to afford her flight back to New Zealand.

On a whim she messaged Curt who, coincidentally, was at his parents' house 350 kilometres away in Brisbane, recovering from an ankle reconstruction following a rugby mishap. 'He said, "I'm sitting in my parents' house for four weeks on crutches, come and hang,"' Rachel recalls.

As much as they tried to fight it, the Facebook friends fell in love over the month they spent together in Brisbane. Even so, Rachel says they knew there wasn't much chance of it working: she'd finally been offered a five-year placement to study medicine – her childhood dream – at the University of Otago, while Curt's career in the Australian Army was also taking off.

Fate looked like it might intervene when Rachel was offered a job as an assistant producer on a kids' science show on Channel 10. They talked about renting a house together, but Curt insisted Rachel head home and fulfil her ambition of becoming a doctor. 'He said I'd resent him if I didn't go back and try,' she says.

Rachel complied, but just a week later, at the beginning of 2012, a lovesick Curt turned up on her doorstep in Dunedin. There was no point fighting their feelings. 'I sat him down and said, "We have to do this long distance,"' Rachel recalls. 'It turned out he was as crazy as me. Crazy because he agreed.'

Just a few months later Curt received orders to go to Afghanistan, as one of ninety combat engineers tasked with searching for IEDs. When he told Rachel, the reality of his chosen profession suddenly chilled her to the bone. She knew the DIY bombs her boyfriend was being sent to find were responsible for more than half the Coalition casualties in Afghanistan. 'I'd watched a British documentary about combat engineers and a lot of them ended up as amputees due to IEDs,' she explains.

Rachel felt solemn and scared as she flew to Australia to farewell Curt. As she sat on his bed in Brisbane while he organised his gear, she ushered the elephant into the room.

'What if you lose your legs?'

After a short pause, Curt replied in a cheery voice, 'I'll just go to the Paralympics.'

'Curt! You can't just say that!' Rachel chided. 'It's a really big deal. Have you actually thought what it means if you lose your legs? You're not taking it seriously.'

Curt was too focused on what lay ahead to pay any mind to hypotheticals. Rachel, on the other hand, couldn't stop thinking about it and she knew there were eighty-nine other families around Australia who felt the same fear. She tried to take comfort in the fact she and Curt were not alone. Besides, Curt even had a card up his sleeve: he'd been appointed unofficial team medic and been given combat first-aid training. The med student in her knew that counted for something.

Three months later Curt was on patrol in Uruzgan Province in south-central Afghanistan when it happened.

He never heard a thing – not a click nor a bang – nor did he see a flash of light when he stepped on the pressure plate of the bomb buried in the soil. One moment he was upright, the next he was on his back in a cloud of falling debris.

Curt's left leg had been blown off below the knee, his right leg at the knee. The blast shattered his wrist, burned his left arm, perforated his eardrums and tore open the back of his thigh. His steel rifle had been snapped in half.

Then his training kicked in. Lying next to a blood-soaked blast crater, Curt coordinated his own salvation, instructing comrades on how to apply the tourniquets he hoped would keep him alive long enough for a medevac flight to reach them.

As Curt was stretchered towards a landing zone for the incoming helicopter he tried to remain upbeat for his shocked and traumatised mates. 'I'll be all good, boys,' he said. 'You'll see me at the Paralympics! But it won't be in the green and gold, I'll be in the black and white of New Zealand.'

Black humour can be a soldier's friend, and the diggers in Curt's unit returned it in spades as their mate clung precariously to life. 'Oh, I suppose you can walk to the chopper then?' one of his stretcher-bearers replied cheekily, threatening to set Curt back on the ground.

Rachel was on a rural medicine placement in Invercargill, the southernmost city in New Zealand's South Island, when the phone woke her early at the backpackers' hostel. Oddly, it was Curt's number that flashed on the screen. Still half asleep, Rachel wandered out into the cold corridor, half expecting to hear his voice, but it was his mum, Kim, on the other end. She was calling from Curt's home phone in Brisbane and barely spoke two words before Rachel's brain caught up with what was happening.

'Oh, Rachel . . .'

'She said, "He's lost his legs and he's critical, and there is a chance he may not live,"' Rachel recounts. 'She said, "It's very touch and go, and we're just waiting for updates."'

Rachel remained numbly composed despite being cold and alone in the draughty hallway. 'I realised I'd wandered down the corridor and I didn't have my contact lenses in,' she says. 'I'm very short-sighted and I thought, "Shit, I don't know where my room is! I can't read the numbers. I don't know where I am. I'm freezing cold in a nightie."'

Rachel banged on a random door, which, fortunately, belonged to two kindly med students in their thirties. 'Excuse me,' she began, 'I'm really sorry to wake you up, but my boyfriend has just lost his legs in Afghanistan and I think I might need some help, but I'm not really sure what that means.'

Then she threw up. With her emotions strangely blunted, Rachel called Tyson, and Curt's other friends, holding it together as they fell apart at the other end of the phone line. 'That was really hard, because they were so upset,' Rachel remembers. 'They were all crying and I felt bad because I wasn't.'

Shock had insulated her from the enormity of the situation.

With her parents on holiday in Adelaide, Rachel called some family friends, Paul and Jocelyn, who live in the isolated town of Gore in the South Island, and asked if she could stay with them for the night. She knew she needed to be somewhere other than a backpackers' hostel to field the horrible phone calls and try to wrap her head around what was happening.

That night Rachel was touched to discover that Paul and Jocelyn had organised a distraction from the awful reality. 'They were so nice,' she says, smiling. 'They'd hired a movie called *Salmon Fishing in the Yemen*, thinking it was a story about fishing and love.' But Rachel had seen it and knew that halfway through, the boyfriend of one of the characters gets deployed to Afghanistan and goes missing.

'Inside I was thinking, "This is kind of hilarious!"' Rachel recalls. 'It was just the state of mind I was in. We sat down to watch it together and I knew the scene was coming up, and that they would start twigging to it, so I said, "I've just got some phone calls to make," and left the room. I told them about it later and laughed about it. I just didn't want them to be upset.'

There's that black humour.

The next day, Rachel and Curt's friends gathered at Tyson's place in Queenstown for tequila shots and camaraderie – exactly what they needed. 'It was really good. We just hung out and talked about how we were going to get through this and support Curt,' says Rachel. Soon Curt's mates were planning a glorious sporting future for him. 'Already they were saying, "We're going to the Rio Paralympics! This is going to be awesome!"'

Although appreciative of the love and the can-do sentiment, Rachel was also cautious and protective of Curt. She asked the guys not to push the Paralympics thing too much. While she thought it was okay to mention it, she also worried it would place a huge expectation on Curt. 'Just remember,' she cautioned, 'he has to learn to walk again first.'

Rachel had no idea Curt was already miles ahead of them all, or that he'd pledged to his brothers in arms they'd soon see him chase greatness on the world stage. He'd been airlifted to an American medical base in Germany for the first of many surgeries, this one to tidy up his wounds and remove the bulk of the blast debris.

He was incredibly lucky to be alive, saved by his calmness on the day and also by his height. The bomb caused a massive penetrating wound to his right leg. Had Curt been any shorter than 6'4" it would have blown apart a major artery in his pelvis, with no way to stop the bleeding. Curt was the tallest soldier in his squad that day, and the only one who could have survived such an explosion.

Rachel was desperate to join him in Germany but Curt's parents convinced her it was wiser to fly to Australia. That way, they said, she wouldn't be jet-lagged and could be there to meet him as soon as he arrived. Rachel packed her bags and headed to Brisbane. One week after Curt was injured, hers was the first face he saw when the plane door opened.

Curt spent the next three months at the Royal Brisbane Hospital and Greenslopes Private Hospital. There were more operations – plastic surgery and microsurgery – as doctors tried to clean and patch the damage done by the IED. Wounds needed to be cleaned and closed, burns required treatment and skin grafts were carried out. The barrage of medical procedures was just the beginning of a long and painful journey, for both of them.

'The only time I nearly fainted was the first time they took the bandages off,' Rachel remembers. 'I could see his legs for the first time and that was really confronting.'

They were Curt's injuries, though, not hers, and Rachel felt powerless in the face of her overwhelming desire to help him recover. Curt, and medical science, would carry the bulk of that load, so Rachel looked for other ways to support him. 'Curt was so strong during that time,' she explains. 'It was really about working out goals for him and trying to find ways to help him get there.'

In the beginning this included practical measures such as learning how to roll Curt onto his side, changing the bedsheets, applying cold packs to his traumatised body and shaving the face she so completely adored. 'It's really, *really* hard to actually feel like you're doing much,' Rachel admits. 'But sometimes I think just being there and going through it together means the most. Showing up each day is enough.'

As if exchanging a baton in a never-ending marathon, there were times Curt needed Rachel to take the lead. One such shift came three weeks after the bomb went off, when Curt got out of bed on his own for the first time. The couple had asked the physiotherapists to mark the milestone with a photograph, but Rachel noticed a change. 'Curt was acting really weirdly,' she recalls. 'I knew something just wasn't right.'

Curt had never moved himself into a wheelchair without assistance before. In that moment – smile! Cameras ready! – it suddenly occurred to him, for perhaps the first time, that he was now a disabled person.

'It hadn't clicked for me that this is obviously a bigger moment for him than I thought, because he'd handled everything so well to that point,' Rachel explains. 'We had this photo taken and then, immediately after, he just broke down. The physios looked at each other and then started slinking out of the room like cats and I thought, "Don't leave me! I don't know what to say!"'

Completely unprepared, Rachel could only hold Curt's hand and tell him it was okay. 'It's hard,' she says of moments like that. 'It's *really* hard and you don't want to say the wrong thing. But once again, I think just being there is really important.'

Seeing such a strong and active man brought low was confronting for Rachel. Before Afghanistan, Curt ran 10 kilometres every afternoon. 'He was so fit!' she says. 'So he'd gone from a super, super fit twenty-something man to a disabled, injured person. Of course he was still Curt, still the same man I loved, but things had changed.'

Now, even in the most unexpected ways, their roles had been reversed. Curt had always been the one to look after Rachel. Now she was driving the car, reaching the top shelves at the supermarket, helping him shower and pushing his wheelchair while his broken arm healed.

It was challenging but Rachel says necessity recast their relationship in a different light. 'I was dating this incredibly handsome, wonderful guy and realised I didn't need the other stuff to love him,' she says. 'We were together because we loved each other, not just twenty-somethings who were attracted to one another.'

They resolved to look for joy in the small moments, and hung on to their shared sense of humour. 'One day we thought getting outside for some fresh air would be good for the both of us, even if it was just out the front door of the hospital,' says Rachel. 'The sun was glorious and it made me break into song with the first lines of "Circle of Life" from *The Lion King*. Oh gosh! We must have looked ridiculous, but I guess being together and then feeling the fresh air was a little euphoric, and fun! We made our own fun along the way.'

Silly songs and trips to the hospital grounds progressed to date nights. The first time they had a chance to hit the town for the evening, while Curt was getting fitted for prosthetics in Sydney, Rachel thought a movie would be a good place to start. They zeroed in on an evening screening of the new Bond movie at the time, *Skyfall*. Anxious to make the night as comfortable as possible for Curt, Rachel booked gold-class seats. The premium section, however, was down a flight of stairs from the theatre entrance.

Descending with the wheelchair was fine but, after 007 had won the day and the credits had rolled, Rachel realised she couldn't push Curt back *up* the stairs.

'I hadn't thought about it!' she says. 'He was too heavy! So he just got out of his wheelchair and, kind of like a mountain gorilla, *climbed* out of the cinema. Everyone was looking at us and I just thought, "Oh my gosh. Oh wow!"'

When Curt made it to the top and hauled himself back into the wheelchair, he looked up at Rachel. 'Sorry,' he said. 'Was that embarrassing?'

'I didn't even know what the word for it was,' Rachel recalls, laughing loudly. 'Truth be told, maybe I was a little embarrassed, the situation was overwhelming. Everyone was looking at us horrified and affronted. We had simply gone on a date and now a cinema full of people were looking at us with pity and sadness. I didn't know what to think.'

Date night heralded the arrival of another wrinkle in their new world order – other people's perceptions. On their first trip to the supermarket a few weeks later, Rachel felt dozens of eyes boring into them. 'I've never had a pram,' she says. 'But all of a sudden I thought, "This is what it's like! No one moves for you! They just run in front of you!" Curt had really sore legs so I was terrified someone might whack into them.'

On one outing she left Curt alone for a few minutes while she scoured the shelves for an elusive item. When she returned, strangers had started talking to him. Another time a man walked over, handed Curt a one-hundred-dollar note and said, 'Thank you for your service.'

'They must have guessed he was an Afghan vet,' Rachel reasons. 'But I looked at Curt and thought, "I don't know how I can handle this. They pity us so much they're dropping money in your lap." I found it really hard.'

Along with all this, Rachel had to juggle the enormous workload of a medical degree back in New Zealand. 'I had to go and do my exams,' she says, 'so I said to Curt, "I need three weeks. I need to actually go back and do some study so I pass, because if I don't pass I have to resit them in January and then I can't help you over summer." I was so scared about failing. I would bring in a little side table and study while he was delirious on ketamine.'

Rachel studied so hard she ended up getting a distinction and a scholarship. 'I was really stressed about failing,' she says. 'I had the fear of God in me that I wouldn't be able to help Curt in rehab if I flunked.'

With their backs against the wall, the young lovers inspired a win-at-all-costs attitude in one another: for Rachel to pass her exams and Curt to get moving again. Just three months after he took that fateful step in Afghanistan, he started walking again, on prosthetic legs fitted at a clinic in Sydney. It was a huge turning point for both of them, mentally and physically.

'The experience for someone who has grown up in a wheelchair is very different from someone who is not patient with it, who doesn't know how to manoeuvre it and who keeps falling out of it,' Rachel observes. 'That was really difficult for Curt. As soon as he put the legs on we said, "Okay, this is going to be where we're heading." We could see the future, upright and mobile, and that was really useful – a huge step and a really, really lovely moment.'

As soon as Curt stood again for the first time, Rachel shed a tear and threw her arms around him – properly. 'It was so nice to hug standing up,' she says, smiling. 'He looked like himself again, and he could look at himself in the mirror standing. I could see what that meant to him.'

Inspired by the milestone and buoyed by the sparkle of the harbour city, Rachel and Curt couldn't wait to get moving again. 'I think we thought the process of walking again would be much easier,' she says. 'We thought, "We're going to be walking! Let's go to Taronga Zoo next weekend!" Even though he could literally only walk three steps with a handrail either side.'

The zoo date never happened. 'There was a constant readjustment of expectations,' Rachel admits. 'I think both of us were quite young and naïve about the whole process. We were constantly having to scale it back.'

Well, in some areas at least.

In November 2012, three months after the explosion, Curt moved back home with his parents in suburban Brisbane. And then he started training. That promise he'd made to his mates on the battlefield in Afghanistan? He hadn't been joking.

Curt had been a canoeist prior to his injury, so para-canoeing felt like a natural choice of sport. He started training in earnest in 2013 and by 2014 he was the fastest in the world. Although he'd had his eyes on the 2016 Paralympics in Rio de Janeiro, in 2015 organisers scrapped canoeing, forcing Curt to switch to kayaking.

The routine of training was a perfect fit for goal-oriented Curt. 'It also gave him an identity,' Rachel explains. 'When people asked him, "What do you do?" he'd say, "Well I'm actually training for the Paralympics."'

Training gave him his fitness back, too. 'He had deconditioned a lot,' says Rachel. 'Regaining that gave him some self-esteem.'

In 2014 Curt travelled to London to captain Australia at the inaugural Invictus Games, the international sports event for wounded service personnel. He won bronze in swimming and made the finals in archery but gained so much more by meeting other disabled people and seeing that they lived very full lives.

As Curt slowly recalibrated and adjusted to his new life, Rachel got the strong sense he was going to be okay but, as their path ahead reappeared, a fork in the road came into view. Rachel needed to return to New Zealand to complete her degree. Initially they'd planned for Curt to move back with her but his medical support base was in Australia and he'd started training for Rio. That changed everything.

Sometimes it felt like the universe was trying to force Curt and Rachel apart. They'd already spent two years in a long-distance relationship and now they were looking down the barrel of another three years separated. 'When you're twenty-four, three years is a lifetime,' Rachel points out. 'We just thought, "What are we doing?"'

As heartbreaking as it was, they decided to take a break and Rachel flew back to New Zealand. 'He never would have had a problem getting a girlfriend or a wife,' Rachel says, 'so I didn't feel guilty that I'm leaving this guy and he's in a wheelchair. It was just that we didn't want to do three more years long distance – either of us.'

If breaking up had been hard in theory, it was even harder in practice. Rachel and Curt Facetimed on their phones every night and it wasn't long before he flew to New Zealand to visit. 'We weren't really on a break,' says Rachel, laughing. 'We knew we were just going to have to make it work!'

As challenging as long-distance love can be, Rachel says the enforced space probably saved their relationship. The breathing room allowed her to retain her identity beyond the major role she had in Curt's life.

'I'd fly to Australia and do a week of rehab with him and that would be quite full-on and, at times, very emotional,' she says. 'We'd get through it, have that week together and then I'd fly back and go to lectures. My friends all knew what was happening, but they also *didn't* know, so everyone treated me normally.'

Rachel came to think of the back-and-forth between Australia and New Zealand as a 'mental break'. At home she'd forget what it was like to be stared at in shops and theatres, then go back to Australia refreshed to be Curt's girlfriend again. 'I think that was a saving grace for us,' she asserts. 'Because it never felt overwhelming and I never lost sight of who I was.'

While there has been little research on the impact of combat-related physical injuries on the partners of military veterans, according to a study published in the *Disability and Health Journal*, there is no doubt Rachel and Curt's relationship was put under significant strain. 'The only reason I can think of that Curt and I managed to stay together, therefore, is all those situational reasons,' Rachel offers. 'I don't doubt that the love and commitment were there for many other couples, but having the reduced emotional burden together meant all we had to do was stay loving each other. We didn't have to worry about bank repayments, children adjusting, me giving up my job to be a full-time carer. I feel very fortunate that we came out the other end together.'

Not that it was ever easy. Around this time Rachel was assigned her first practical rotation, in vascular surgery at Wellington Hospital. 'They do all the amputations and surgeries for the diabetic patients,' she says. Her new colleagues had no idea what was going on in Rachel's private life. 'I'd be in theatre every day holding up legs while they were being amputated, and my team didn't know!' she reveals. 'I didn't tell them because I didn't know how to. So I would hold on to the leg while the surgeon sawed it off, and you have to watch out for the stray bone chips and then you carry the leg and put it in the bin.'

Unsurprisingly, Rachel's mental health suffered and her nightly dreams became populated by people with no legs. 'During the day I'm holding legs while they're amputated,' she says. 'I'm carrying legs! My boyfriend has no legs! Why is my life now full of legs that aren't attached to bodies?'

Like soldiers, medicos share a dark sense of humour to help cushion them from the trauma inherent in their work. Rachel heard a lot of black jokes in the operating theatre, and took it in her stride. 'It was a hospital and so it's not offensive, which I understood at the time,' she says. 'But it was really hard.'

On the last day of her five-week rotation, Rachel baked muffins and took them to work. 'I said, "Hey, funny story – I actually know a bit about amputations and care of stumps. My boyfriend lost his legs in Afghanistan six months ago." There was complete radio silence.'

After she returned to university the following week, Rachel started hearing the first frantic phone call from Curt's mum playing over and over in her mind. 'I'd be in lectures and it would be really invasive,' she recalls. 'I didn't really pick up on the fact that if you put that stuff together it can fall under the category of mild PTSD.'

Rachel approached the university dean and told her the phantom phone calls were making it hard for her to focus in lectures. 'The dean is a psychiatrist,' says Rachel. 'She looked at me and said, "Rachel, you've done your psychiatry block. Doesn't this ring any bells?"'

From the beginning Rachel had rejected the notion she was in any way wounded by what had happened to Curt. 'I said, "But it wasn't me! I wasn't there! I can't have any trauma. Picking up a phone isn't trauma!"'

The dean explained how the phone call was most likely the event Rachel's brain had attached to the immense sorrow and upheaval she'd undergone. 'PTSD was very much a word associated with soldiers,' Rachel says. 'I didn't identify as having PTSD but I know I had symptoms which showed I'd been through trauma. I'd started to develop things which were just my body's way of saying the last three months have been really stressful and I'm trying to understand everything.'

It's only in the last decade that clinicians have become more aware of what's now called post-intensive care syndrome – family (PICS-F). The term describes psychological problems observed in family members of ICU patients: anxiety, depression, complicated grief and PTSD.

Post-intensive care syndrome affects as many as 50 per cent of ICU survivors. The number affected by PICS-F may be even higher. The American Association of Critical-Care Nurses found that 10 to 75 per cent of survivors' families had a member who experienced anxiety, and that up to 42 per cent of families showed symptoms of PTSD. Upon a patient's discharge, one-third of families had a member who was taking medications for depression or anxiety.

And as we deal with the fallout of the pandemic, PICS-F may be the next public health crisis we face, according to America's National Institute of Health. Due to the infectious nature of COVID-19, ICU patients have been isolated, and family visits restricted or banned altogether, burdening families and healthcare workers exponentially.

Thankfully clinicians are now researching how to best mitigate PICS-F, help families get through the trauma of having a loved one in hospital and manage afterwards. Measures include daily family care rituals, real-time communication and diaries that both nurses and family members can update.

Rachel says she could have benefited from this kind of intervention. She was incredibly lonely during Curt's time in hospital and also afterwards. Although they had great friends, none of them truly understood what she and Curt were going through, so there weren't many people she could talk to.

Rachel soon recognised the importance of self-care. 'To look after someone else, you have to look after yourself,' she points out. She ensured she covered the basics such as sleep, eating well, watching her alcohol intake, putting on regular clothes and occasionally treating herself to a spa day, or anything that helped her relax.

'I vomited constantly for the first ten days after Curt got injured, probably from stress and shock,' she says.

'Having regular small meals and ultimately getting anti-nausea medication was necessary and all part of the bigger picture of not forgetting to look after myself. I was no help to anyone, including myself, when I had to run out of Curt's room in the hospital to vomit in the visitor toilets.'

And she learned to let her emotions be. 'When you get sad, be sad,' she says simply. 'When you need to cry, let it all out. It's okay to sit in the rubble and feel broken; the dust will eventually settle and you will be able to get up again. If you don't allow yourself that process of working through the grief it makes it much harder in the long run.'

Rachel's advice to anyone with a loved one impacted by a major injury or traumatic life event is 'maintain your identity'. 'Being defined by something that happened to you can erode your sense of self, and you lose perspective on who you are and the things that bring happiness to you,' she explains. 'Make sure you set boundaries with yourself, and with your friends and family, so there is always time in the day where the conversation isn't around "the event", and that you make a conscious effort to continue some kind of normalcy despite the chaos. It could be continuing to go to your same gym class, making time to read that novel on your bedside table or going out for dinner with friends where the conversation is as close to normal as possible. Life has to go on.'

Rachel has re-read some of the text messages she and Curt exchanged soon after he was injured. They talked about where they'd live and how they'd build a future together despite what had happened. 'On the first day I met Curt, and promptly ran away, I thought to myself he was the guy I would marry,' Rachel affirms. 'And that did not change at all for me.'

Rachel doesn't pretend they haven't sacrificed a lot to stay together – something she struggled with in the beginning. 'I used to try and push him to do things which we used to do together to prove we could still do it,' she confesses. 'Then it would be so stressful and awful that you kind of lose sight of how your relationship was or who you are.'

The solution lay in adjusting expectations. 'I think as soon as I started to realign and say, "Okay, what *can* we do together, what do we enjoy doing together?" then I could reframe our relationship and build it into something else and try and keep some of the things we had before. Then, when we could finally see a little further along – maybe even around the corner – the future came back into focus.'

Still, as those text messages from the early days testify, some massive questions remained.

'Were we going to have kids?'

'How would Curt be with a toddler?'

Early on, the Paralympics weren't squarely on the table, and neither Rachel nor Curt could see what a career might look like for him.

'Is he going to have a job?'

'Am I going to work while he's at home?'

Time, and Curt's focus and drive, provided the answers. As he built his identity as an amputee and sportsman, a new career took shape: athlete and motivational speaker. Sport also became Curt's medicine and therapy. Less than two years after he lost his legs, he competed at a national level in sprint canoe. He won gold at the 2014 World Championships and came home with a gold medal for Australia from the 2016 Paralympics in Rio – the promise to his army mates fulfilled. He has also taken part in four Invictus Games.

Each milestone brought Rachel and Curt a greater understanding of the bigger picture, and life's amazing possibilities. 'We met people who had been injured like Curt, or worse,' says Rachel. 'Some of these couples had kids and so we looked at their relationships. If they were married, maybe five years in front of us in life, we could see they had very happy lives and then start to picture that was potentially where we could go.'

Rachel says talking to people who've been through a similar experience is invaluable. 'Find these people, your trauma mentors,' she advises. 'There's often an online support group or network for most situations or experiences. Reach out!'

She feels privileged to meet Paralympians and soldiers who've come out the other side of life-altering trauma. 'People survive a lot,' she says. 'It takes a while, though. One thing I learned early on is to change your expectations and just make the timeframe a bit longer. That doesn't mean you're not going to have the same ending, but just take it slow. Take a deep breath. Take every day as it comes and you will get through.'

Not even the pandemic could stand in their way. As the rest of the world locked down, Curt won two gold medals at the 2020 Paralympics in Tokyo. And today Doctor Rachel Martin is in her dream job in the Intensive Care Unit at Royal Brisbane Hospital.

Together they have learned that good can come from change – you just have to look for it.

Rachel says Curt's injury has taught him patience because now he has to take the time to put on his legs if he wants to do anything. He's more tolerant, too. 'Tolerant of pain and being uncomfortable, which I'm very aware of,' she says. 'He's uncomfortable and hot and sore most days.'

Curt's patience and tolerance have rubbed off on Rachel, too. 'I think being tolerant and being aware of others has definitely made me a different doctor,' she says. Her job often requires her to tell people's families and friends that something awful has happened and, despite everything doctors have done, their loved one will never be the same again. 'I take that *extremely* seriously,' she says. 'I know how much power is in those words because I can remember exactly what was said to me. "He's lost his legs and he's critical. There is a chance he may not live." Those words haunted me for months.'

Not so much nowadays.

My husband, John, and I have been blessed to become close friends with this amazing young couple. When they tied the knot in June 2019 we were honoured to be among the people to share their special day. I think about Rachel and Curt often and I hope all of their dreams come true: renovating a house and having a couple of kids. At the time of writing I was delighted to learn they'd made a start by becoming proud owners of a gorgeous golden retriever puppy named Theo.

Six

Chloe

Chloe Kennedy's life was brimming over with happiness and fulfillment in early 2017. She'd just turned twenty-eight, she'd recently fallen in love and she was making the most of living and working in Italy, where she'd moved the previous year to learn the language and cuisine. The view from a snow-capped peak in Baranci on the morning of 13 February was too glorious not to share. Chloe panned her phone around the shimmering mountains as she Facetimed her mum, Robyn, and boyfriend, Antonello, back in Australia. 'Look at this!' she exclaimed as sunlight glinted off the ranges.

The active and vivacious young woman from Sydney's western suburbs had trekked into the Dolomites with her friend Angelo for a day of skiing near the village of San Candido. It was a crystal-clear morning, almost spring-time in Italy, although unbeknown to Chloe the bottom of the hill she would be skiing down was shrouded in fog. After Chloe clicked one more selfie in the sunshine, she launched down the slope. Unable to see through the mist that enveloped her, the last thing she remembers is being catapulted forward.

Then, nothing.

'I don't know if I lost my memory when I hit my head or if I've repressed it,' Chloe says. 'But I'm glad I don't remember. I'd rather not relive that part.'

She'd fallen about halfway down the slope and lay motionless in the snow. An emergency medical team care-fully brought her down from the mountainside and rushed her to the San Maurizio Hospital in Bolzano, where she spent the next eight days on life support in a medically induced coma. With Chloe's life suspended in a sedated void, surgeons operated to fuse her broken neck. They used a metal plate to stabilise her spine but knew she would never walk again.

*

I've encountered a lot of tragedy over the years. In my line of work, getting up close and personal with other people's heartbreak is an occupational hazard. Each and every story I've covered about suffering or loss has left its mark on me, but there was an element of Chloe's misfortune that touched me especially deeply.

Fate can be cruel, but it can seem dreadfully so when it intervenes in the prime of life. When disaster struck Chloe, she was so vital, and so full of hope and promise. Perhaps I felt for her so keenly because she reminded me of how I'd been at twenty-eight.

I often thought about Chloe after COVID stopped the world. Because my own children were blossoming into adulthood, I'd become particularly mindful of the pandemic's impact on the twenty-somethings of society. In a way it seemed like they had the most to lose as their upward trajectories were suddenly grounded by a microscopic germ.

Knowing how stoically Chloe had dealt with traumatic upheaval, I was eager to get her take on how people can recover and rebuild when their dynamic and active lives are suddenly rendered motionless.

Chloe was six months pregnant when we met. I was working on a story for *Sunday Night* about women with quadriplegia following the challenging road to motherhood. I was in the theatre when a doctor lifted Chloe's baby daughter,

Aurora, from her womb and passed her to her beaming dad, Antonello. It was an enormous privilege and such an incredible moment to behold that I don't have the words to properly describe how I felt. I do, however, recall bursting into tears when Aurora took her first breath. We all did.

As the tiny newborn rested in her father's arms, I had a powerful sense that every dream and adventure was hers for the taking. Aurora would grow up under the guidance of parents who were overflowing with love and positivity. And she will know resilience because her mum wrote the book on it.

Chloe Kennedy is, hands down, one of the sunniest people I've ever had the pleasure to meet. Her face is framed by a striking mass of auburn hair, she has a laugh you can hear from next door and she possesses one of those smiles you can't help but mirror. I only had to spend five minutes with her to understand she wasn't one to watch life pass by from the sidelines or let anything slow her down. After witnessing the birth of her baby girl, I also knew they'd be part of my life forever. Our time together had been too intimate and emotional for me to simply say good luck and goodbye. In my heart I feel like Aurora's fairy godmother, and I take great joy in seeing her grow.

After Chloe agreed to share her story we decided to start at the beginning of her 'new life', when she regained consciousness in the Italian hospital eight days after her accident. She had no idea she'd undergone emergency surgery on her spine and when she came to she was confused to see Antonello at her bedside along with her mum, Robyn, and sisters, Kim, Kylie and Renee. They'd made an emotional and stressful dash from Sydney after Chloe's skiing buddy Angelo had phoned to tell them she was in a critical condition and might not live.

After a week of heavy sedation, Chloe was still in a medicated haze when an Italian doctor sat by her bed and delivered the prognosis. She remembers him speaking but says the words didn't really sink in. It was Renee who gently broached the nature of Chloe's spinal injury with her. She tried to sound as positive as she could for her little sister. 'It's good where you've damaged it,' Renee said. 'It could have been worse.'

Renee's loving default to tenderness and reassurance had left Chloe feeling hopeful. 'I remember thinking, "I've come out of this really lucky! I'll just be in bed for a while healing and everything will be fine."'

Chloe had fractured the C6 vertebra in the base of her neck. One saving grace was the fact her spinal cord wasn't severed, which meant that while she was paralysed below the chest, she retained movement in her arms and wrists.

'You hear words like "quadriplegic, paraplegic, paralysis",' Chloe says. 'And I just thought, "That's not me because I can feel my body. I just need to be in bed for a while and then everything will be fine."'

Chloe was still trying to absorb the fact she was paralysed when she was flown to Sydney aboard a specially equipped medevac plane two weeks later. The journey home was an ordeal, and a harbinger of the difficulties she was likely to face in the future. She was gently stretchered onto the small chartered jet, still connected to machines that were keeping her alive. She had a tracheostomy tube to help her breathe and a feeding tube down her throat. An anaesthetist and a doctor were onboard, plus five pilots on rotation for the twenty-seven-hour flight to Australia. Antonello and Robyn were by her side the whole way.

Upon touchdown in Mascot, Chloe was taken directly to Royal North Shore Hospital for a month-long stay, with the first two days in the Intensive Care Unit. There, doctors removed her tracheostomy tube and monitored her closely to ensure she could breathe on her own. Once she was stable she was moved into a room and a degree of routine.

Food and medication were administered via a tube. Chloe was dosed with multiple painkillers, antispasmodic drugs and an antidepressant. It was the latter that Chloe questioned. 'I wanted to know why I was on an antidepressant,' she says. 'I said, "I know my situation. I'd rather come to terms with that on my own with a clear mind."'

With hindsight Chloe realises that defiant attitude and belief in her emotional strength at the time 'was probably a mistake'.

As doctors gradually reduced her dose, the full weight of Chloe's reality pressed down hard on her. She remembers sobbing and asking, 'Is this my life?'

'My family wasn't there,' she recalls. 'Antonello wasn't there, I had just been in Italy being very independent and then all of a sudden I'm wondering, "What has happened?"'

Chloe says these were among her darkest days. 'I couldn't move myself in bed, I couldn't feed myself, I couldn't really do much. That was very daunting.'

After stabilising for four weeks she was transferred to Prince of Wales Hospital for eight gruelling months of intense rehabilitation. The daily grind brought her new future into sharp focus. 'This *is* my life,' Chloe remembers thinking. 'I started to realise there were things that I was not going to be able to do like I did before.'

With acceptance now part of her emotional outlook, Chloe threw herself into rehabilitation. It was physically and mentally exhausting, at times tedious, at other times frustrating, and Chloe struggled to keep her expectations in check. She desperately tried to hang on to hope but was so often pushed back by reality. 'In rehab they don't say, "Oh, you will be able to do this," or, "You'll be able to do that," but they also don't *stop* you from doing anything,' she explains. 'They just want you to be as independent and functional as you can be.'

Rehab, however, delivered Chloe one small comfort. She remembers a guy who was in the bed next to hers. He was about the same age, with a similar injury. 'I was sad for him,' she says. 'I was sad for both of us but I found it reassuring to know I wasn't the only one.'

Chloe – who admits to having an 'overachieving personality' – grappled with the physiotherapy and was frustrated she wasn't improving fast enough. The end goal was to get as much movement in her arms as possible. 'I couldn't do things for myself. I had a different expectation to what was reality,' she says.

Her mum, Robyn, was constantly by her side, helping her push that little bit harder. The sessions with the occupational therapist frustrated Chloe just as much as the physiotherapy, as they spent endless hours and days focusing on trying to train her fingers to pinch.

While Chloe is technically a quadriplegic (because all four limbs are affected), the fact her spinal cord is intact means she has some limited feeling in her body. She can sense touch but not temperature or pain, the upper part of her arms work and there's movement in her wrists, but her hands are partially paralysed. She can't stand on her own, but with assistance and a walking frame can manage the smallest of movements in her legs.

In the final months of rehab, Chloe turned her mind to life outside the nurturing, protective bubble of hospitals. On weekends she'd take daytrips with Antonello to hunt for an apartment that was wheelchair friendly. It was a stressful time but in November 2017 – nearly two years after she'd bounded off to begin her grand adventure abroad – Chloe finally came home, in a wheelchair.

When she moved into a new apartment in Zetland with Antonello, she realised leaving the safety of the medical system wasn't as daunting or frightening as she'd feared. 'I was happy to finally be out of hospital and try to get a normal life, or my new normal, so I guess that overtook things,' she says. 'The anticipation was worse than the reality.'

As medicos were no longer on call, Antonello stepped up to fill the void both emotionally and physically. 'He's done things that a boyfriend should not have to do for their partner,' Chloe says. 'But he does, and I say to him, "No, you're my boyfriend! Don't! You shouldn't see this." And he's like, "Don't be stupid, just come here."'

Chloe was keenly aware it wasn't only her life that had been significantly reshaped. Racked with guilt, she gave Antonello the option of walking away to make a life for himself with somebody else. After all, they'd become a couple just eight months before Chloe embarked on her European odyssey.

Chloe had always been the responsible type. She excelled at school before studying medical science at university for three years. She'd taken up her dream job with the Australian Red Cross, conducting tissue matching in the solid organ transplantation lab, but then the time came to finally take the gap year she'd denied herself in favour of studying hard. 'I thought it was my time to just do something for me,' she tells me, smiling.

A lover of good food, Chloe planned to travel for a while then base herself in Florence to do a culinary course and work as an intern chef. 'I didn't want to be a chef for the rest of my life or work in a kitchen, but I just wanted a change,' she says.

To do that properly she figured she'd need to at least try to learn the language. A girlfriend suggested Chloe buy her coffee from the cute Italian barista at their local café in Sydney's Beaconsfield, just around the corner from work, and ask him to teach her a few key phrases.

Antonello was more than happy to tutor the gorgeous

new customer. They swapped phone numbers and arranged to meet for ice-cream. The Italian lessons never transpired but the language of love quickly drew them together. Nevertheless, Chloe was determined to push ahead with her trip. So, less than a year later, Antonello waved her goodbye at Sydney Airport.

Just as smitten as Chloe, Antonello flew around the world to join her in July 2016, and introduced her to family and friends in his hometown of Lido di Fermo in Marche. They spent a glorious month together relishing family dinners, days at the beach, dining out with friends and travelling before Antonello returned to Sydney and Chloe continued her adventure.

She immersed herself in culinary school and language classes before taking on her first internship. But with her visa expiry date looming in March, Chloe decided to wrap up work a little earlier than planned and pack as much travel in as she could before it was time to come home. She wanted to take in the Carnival of Venice en route to Iceland, Sweden and Finland to see the aurora borealis, or northern lights – but not before a spot of skiing in the Dolomites.

The accident – just eighteen months after they first met – brought the relationship into sharp relief for Chloe. She knew that life with a disabled woman wasn't what Antonello had imagined when they met. 'I didn't want to be that selfish person making him stay with me if that's not what he wanted to do one hundred per cent,' Chloe explains. 'I told him I'd be fine, and he was free to go.'

Leaving was never an option for Antonello. 'He *always* says that to me,' Chloe confides softly. 'He says, "What's different? You were Chloe before and you're Chloe now. You've still got your brain and you're still you, just things are a little bit different." He's really good at reminding me of that and he has never wanted out. He has never questioned our relationship or his commitment.'

Antonello's commitment gave Chloe the belief that a version of the life she had planned was within reach.

We heard the phrase 'the new normal' a lot during the pandemic, and for someone whose life has changed so dramatically, I notice Chloe uses the word 'normal' a lot. Not in the new COVID-affected sense, though, but in the sense of resuming some semblance of their old life.

They love to socialise, although they prefer dinner parties at home to trying to navigate a restaurant that isn't wheelchair friendly. Chloe resumed work, too. She'd volunteered in the genetics diagnostic department at Prince of Wales Hospital while she was a rehab inpatient, so when she was discharged it was an easy progression into more hours.

As 'normality' took root in other aspects of life, Chloe and Antonello were also determined to push ahead with another life phase they'd envisaged – having a family. Chloe may have been in a wheelchair, and certain things were a lot harder, but this didn't mean their dream was derailed.

'Having a family was always something in my mind after my accident,' she says. In fact it was one of the first things she asked her nurse while she was lying motionless in her hospital bed in Italy. 'I think I really confused her because I tried to ask, "Can I still have babies?"' Chloe remembers. 'And I think she thought that I thought I'd *had* a baby. So I was like, "No-no-no! Am I still able to be pregnant and have children?"'

Chloe's scrappy Italian finally cut through. Once the nurse understood, she smiled and said, 'Yes, there's no reason why you can't.'

When the couple discussed the idea of parenthood back in Australia, Chloe's doctor agreed that pregnancy and childbirth would pose no major problems for her. Having received the blessing of medicos, it was time for a conversation with Chloe's mum, Robyn. Would she be able to give them the extra help they were no doubt going to need? The answer, through tears of happiness, was 'Of course!'

Chloe says she fell pregnant easily and naturally. She laughs uproariously when she addresses 'the big question'.

'A thing people ask or I know they *want* to ask is, "You're in a wheelchair – can you have sex?"' she says. 'Well, yes! Everything still works like it did before – maybe a little bit different – but I can still have sex and I can still make a baby the way other women do.'

Her pregnancy was smooth sailing, just like she'd been assured. There are no extra complications for a woman with Chloe's condition other than limited space in the womb and a bit of extra discomfort. A woman in a wheelchair can potentially have less room between her thorax and pelvis, so the area may be a little more compressed, but there is no adverse effect on the baby or the mother's long-term health.

Chloe had also been told there was the possibility of a vaginal delivery. The uterus contains muscle fibres that operate involuntarily, unlike the skeletal muscles in our legs and arms, which are consciously controlled. One concern, however, is that someone with quadriplegia can go into labour and not know it or feel it. There's also a high level of skill required from the anaesthetist to ensure the anaesthetic is working if a patient can't tell them if they can feel it or not. Even though a patient may not directly sense pain, their body can trigger a nervous-system response such as autonomic dysreflexia, which causes dangerously high blood pressure and potential cardiac arrest.

After weighing everything up, Chloe and her obstetrician agreed a caesarean section was the safest option. One thing medical science couldn't control, however, was Chloe's emotional state. As her pregnancy progressed she oscillated between feeling happy and excited, and fearful and guilty. Chloe fretted she was being 'selfish' and potentially putting her own desire to be a mum ahead of her child's needs. She also feared she wouldn't be a capable mother; that she'd be unable to do certain things and be too scared to pick up her baby.

Always one to reach for the positive in life, however, Chloe knew deep down these were challenges she *could* face; she'd just need some extra help. She determined to focus on what she could do, not what she couldn't. And what she could do was hold her baby and love her.

Both of us, though, were more than a little nervous about capturing all of this on camera! From the moment I met her, I knew how important it was for Chloe to give other women hope. That's why she was so open to sharing her story. I'll be honest, though, I'd never actually seen a woman give birth. I've had two babies, but I was too busy pushing to watch, let alone take notes.

When the day came, the camera crew and I scrubbed and gowned up, and took our place in the corner of the theatre where we wouldn't get in the way. I will admit to closing my eyes as the doctor made the first cut into Chloe's belly, but what followed was an incredibly powerful and emotional experience.

Chloe and Antonello's beautiful, healthy baby girl was born on 13 June 2019 in Sydney's Royal Hospital for Women, a little over two years after Chloe's accident. They named her Aurora after the northern lights Chloe had been so excited to see but was denied by fate. 'Antonello was the one who came up with the name,' Chloe says. 'It's got a lot of meaning for me.'

Antonello let me hold his precious daughter within moments of her birth. When she was bundled up safely, I clearly remember looking at her tiny face and being overwhelmed by the amount of love that was coming her way. I visited them at home a few weeks later and was delighted to see Chloe already doing so well and Antonello clucking about with pride.

Most mums struggle the first time around; I know I did. Few mothers have any idea what they're doing and swing between overwhelming love and immense fear on any given day. There are sleepless nights and there's so much to learn. Like most people I'd never even changed a nappy before my son was born.

Then there's the apprehension that comes with holding such a tiny, precious bundle of a baby. My firstborn was so delicate, wriggly, floppy and vulnerable that I was terrified I'd drop him. The nerves surrounding this were much more intense for Chloe, of course. Mindful of her lack of strength and absence of grip, she always had someone with her when she picked Aurora up – and that was just the beginning.

With no dexterity in her fingers, Chloe found something as routine as dressing Aurora an enormous challenge. To overcome it she avoided outfits with buttons and had any clips changed to Velcro. She says there's no way she could have managed those early months without Antonello and Robyn by her side. She also had occasional professional in-home help from Alliance and Hireup.

When COVID-19 appeared in early 2020, agency helpers were no longer allowed to enter her home. With Antonello at work, Chloe often found herself isolated with a nine-month-old baby to look after. Necessity, she says, was the mother of invention. 'It forced me to think outside the box,' she explains. 'You know, "How can I get off the floor? How can I change her nappy?"'

Looking around at what she had at her disposal, Chloe discovered she could use the bath lifter – a remote-controlled chair designed to lower patients into the bath – to carry some of the load. 'I don't have a bath but I thought, "That will help me get on the floor to play with Aurora and then

I can get up off the floor and just transfer into my chair!"
I was really missing that – she'd be on the floor playing
and I wanted to be on the floor with her.'

After she mastered the lifter, Chloe realised she could use
it to lift Aurora, too. 'I positioned the bath lifter between a
set of drawers and a table so she couldn't fall off and then
I'd guide her onto it, lift her out and she'd crawl onto my
lap!' Chloe says with a satisfied smile.

Ironically, COVID-19 – the plague that stopped the
world – reignited Chloe's life in some regards by making
her more determined and more independent.

Inspired, she began building up her strength. She'd
made good progress in the months after her accident but
she'd put her intense rehab on hold when she conceived.
Chloe started working with a new trainer who helped her
strengthen some essential muscles. 'I've been doing a lot
of standing, but more in terms of keeping my legs strong
to help me with day-to-day tasks,' she explains. 'The goal
isn't walking, the goal is to maintain muscle and strength
because that's what makes up for the weakness in my
upper body.'

Chloe says having some strength in her quadriceps makes
everything easier. 'My transfers are getting better,' she says.
'I'm getting in and out of the car without using slide boards
and without Antonello picking me up and putting me in.

So now we just go to the car, I pull up, maybe if I'm a bit weak he might need to hold my hips a little bit. In general I'm just doing it on my own while he's dealing with getting Aurora into her seat.'

Chloe found it useful to break her myriad challenges down into singular, manageable pieces, like getting in and out of her apartment building. 'You've been to my place,' she says. 'Our front doors are so heavy and I couldn't open them. I gave up and thought I'd just go through the garage instead.'

She has since put the challenge to her trainer. 'I said, "I know what we can work on – my front doors!" So now I can get in both front doors. One of them is a little bit harder but it's actually manageable. And I thought, "Why didn't I do this two years ago?"'

As her strength increases, so does her potential. More confidence in her abilities has led to more independence. Now, in 2022, Chloe savours the chance to have fun and enjoy things any young woman her age would. 'I went to the Hunter Valley a few weekends ago for a friend's hens' and I didn't take a shower chair and I didn't have support workers. I just went on my own and managed everything on my own, showering and dressing independently.' She beams. 'And my sister Renee kept saying, "Do you need help?" And I was like, "No, I'm fine. Just leave me." I've never had that sort of outlook until this year because I know I can be independent.'

Buoyed by her progress, Chloe became keen to share what she has learned with others. She offers tips on how she manages some of life's everyday challenges on a few Facebook quadriplegic support pages, and launched an online retail store called Beyond Adaptive that stocks all of the gadgets that have made her life easier.

'I kept thinking, "Why didn't I know about these products? Why did I have to go out and find all this stuff myself? Why did I have to do the problem-solving?"' she says. 'I'm fine with doing it, but it's only because I'm a motivated person. But what about people who are struggling? That's why I started this business: "I'm going to make it easier for you – here's what could help."'

Items in her catalogue range from helpful kitchen gadgets and a device for doing up buttons and zippers to no-tie laces and even a lap belt that holds a baby securely in place on a mother's lap.

Chloe has also taken others with quadriplegia under her wing, including a man from country New South Wales who broke his neck swimming when he hit a sandbar in December 2020. In her own way she's become what Rachel Martin calls a 'trauma mentor' – a guide to show other patients what the future can look like.

'He's a very similar level to me,' Chloe says. 'His injury is a little bit more complete, where he can't feel his legs, but his arms would be stronger than mine. He's already got a three-year-old and a five-year-old, and his wife is currently pregnant. So I'm just throwing things at him like, "Oh, you need to use this. You need to use that. We're going to make you a cot. Come around for dinner and see what it's like to be out of the hospital."'

These days Chloe juggles her business and support roles with a few other jobs. She's moved on from genetics research into a business development role within NSW Health Pathology. She's also worked with Spinal Cord Injuries Australia, mainly making instructional videos to show others with quadriplegia how she manages to cook and do her hair and make-up.

On top of that she's been employed to help trial a new wheelchair product that creates a pressure map to ensure clients have good weight distribution to help prevent the development of pressure sores. 'And then I've got my little side business, Beyond Adaptive, my own training and being a mum,' she says with a satisfied chuckle.

To hear Chloe talk about her life in such uncomplicated terms sometimes makes it seem like she does it all in a canter. But I know how hard she works and how much she still has on her plate from a medical point of view. Recently she underwent two rounds of throat surgery to rectify a problem in her neck. 'After the accident I was fused from C5 to C7 with a big metal plate and I was having issues swallowing,' she explains. 'It ended up being a lot more involved than surgeons realised, because once they got into my neck they realised that the plate had eroded through my oesophagus and skin had started forming over that.'

After the corrective surgeries Chloe needed to be fed via a tube for a month and was unable to drink, or even suck on an ice cube.

Next she's potentially facing an advanced form of bladder surgery that is becoming more common among those with quadriplegia, particularly women. 'I have a catheter that stays in surgically, all the time, but it gives me hell – lots of urinary tract infections,' she explains. 'With the new surgery they get your appendix and they make a channel from your belly button into your bladder, and you self-catheterise through your belly button! That's how the urine drains!'

Once again she makes something so potentially daunting sound like a walk in the park. 'In one of the support groups that I'm part of, nearly all the girls in America have had this surgery,' Chloe enthuses. 'I've seen photos; you can't even tell! And it means I should get fewer UTIs.'

Every step, be it medical, physical, emotional or professional, makes Chloe stronger and more confident in her most cherished role – motherhood. She and Antonello have even been talking about having another baby. 'Once Aurora is five and in big school I think it'll be easier,' Chloe muses. 'And because little girls like to be mums I think she would actually be helpful. Whereas I could not do a toddler and a newborn.'

One caveat to expanding the family lies not in Aurora's age, but Chloe's. 'I'll be considered a very old mum as far as quadriplegics go,' she says. 'If I wait another three years I'll be thirty-six and my spinal doctor already tells me I'm too old. But if there is a second baby, I know I'd have a lot more confidence.'

In the meantime, Chloe and Antonello have fulfilled other dreams, including returning to Italy together with Aurora. 'We went to see Antonello's grandmother,' says Chloe. 'She's from this tiny little town of two hundred people called Oliveto Lucano. Aurora is her first great-grandchild and the day she was born Antonello's grandma went to the local pub and bought everyone drinks.'

When they showed up with precious Aurora in tow, Antonello's then eighty-eight-year-old grandmother, Felicia, laid down the law. 'She said, "I'm going to die before you guys ever get married so we're going to the jeweller and I'm buying you rings,"' Chloe recalls with a laugh. 'So she bought us wedding rings and she said we have to wear them!'

'Do you think you might get married for real?' I ask.

'Ask Antonello!' Chloe replies in a flash.

As a couple they've already been through so much in their six years together, and the journey has brought about a major change for Antonello as well. Watching and helping Chloe inspired him to alter his career path and he now helps others in similar situations to his partner.

'He's doing disability support work via Hireup,' Chloe says with more than a hint of pride. If someone with a disability needs help, they can call Antonello. 'He likes being his own boss, and when he gets a job, he feels like he's winning. So people will post jobs such as "I need help mowing my lawn" or "I want to build this shed and I don't have the strength or the ability", and he takes on all of those. There's one guy he drives to physio, and he waits for him and drives him wherever he wants, or he'll help him out in his house or take him grocery shopping. He likes those kinds of jobs and he's got a few regular clients now who love him.'

Although she found ways to look after herself during the COVID years, the once fiercely independent Chloe has grown more comfortable about asking for help from others. 'I'm definitely not that person who says, "I don't need help!" If I'm pushing up a hill that's quite hard and a person says, "Do you need a hand?", I'm quick to say,

"Yeah, that'd be great. Thank you." After that, part of me feels I've made that person's day because they're now thinking, "I'm so glad I helped that girl!" So you sort of have to see it in that sense as well.'

It's been a blessing to see little Aurora grow from a newborn into a delightful three-year-old. She has a head full of tight curls, a mischievous grin and big brown eyes. She's cute and cheeky, and chats to her mum in English and her dad in Italian.

It's clear that motherhood grounds Chloe and gives her joy, but she is determined to do other things that bring her happiness, too. She feels it's vital to take time out for herself, away from babies and bath lifters. 'I need to do the things that I like and are important to me for my physical ability but also my mental health,' she stresses. 'I like my business development role because I go to the hospital with people who don't have spinal cord injuries. They treat me just like every other employee and I have the same deadlines and the same work schedule.'

One of her latest passions is wheelchair rugby, aka 'murderball'. Played by teams on a hardwood court, it's a surprisingly brutal mix of rugby, basketball and handball that features plenty of collisions and frequently sees players dislodged from their chairs and sprawled on the floor. 'We're called the Gladiators,' Chloe enthuses with a devilish grin. 'I'm not in the main team or anything – I just play for fun.'

At first she was a spectator, but watching other people in wheelchairs being physical and competitive encouraged Chloe to push herself in her own life. 'It's so good mentally being around other people in similar situations as me, talking about things that you don't talk about with your able-bodied friends,' she says. 'So I do try to make that happen. I'll find babysitters or get Mum to come over or get Antonello to stay home. Not that that comes before Aurora, but it's an important part in my lifestyle. I was an active person before my injury but I didn't necessarily like team sports. Now playing wheelchair rugby is the best thing I ever did.'

It seems like the right moment to ask Chloe what advice, if any, she'd give to someone who reads her chapter – particularly if they've had an injury or are struggling with life in other ways.

She pauses for a few moments to think before answering. 'You need to look a little bit outside the box,' she says. 'Look into other avenues that could make you happy. I hear a lot of people lose their friends after injury or trauma; well, they're obviously not the friends for you. Find other groups. Find things that make you happy in life.'

Chloe also says it's important not to fear change, whether you want it or not. 'I still have certain things that I did before my accident, but I have a lot of new things,' she says. 'I started a different job, a different sport. I still have my partner, my family, a new thing is having my baby. So there's definitely a mixture of my "before life" and my "new life" and putting it all together. Also, think about what are the most important things in your life and just be around other positive people.'

To underscore the point Chloe quotes a meme she recently saw on social media:

'A stranger said to me, "How do you stay so positive when you're in a wheelchair?" And I responded, "How do you stay so negative when you can walk?"'

'I absolutely love that!' she says, and laughs that laugh the neighbours can hear.

Finally, Chloe says we should never give up on our plans and our dreams. 'I still want to see the northern lights,' she points out, smiling. 'But now we can do it as a family.'

Seven

Danny

It has been a time of such loss.

As I write this more than 6.2 million people have died of COVID-19. I think about the tens of millions, if not hundreds of millions of people around the globe who suffered the fallout: the people who were torn apart by the sudden death of a loved one or a dear friend. In Australia, thousands of families have lived through this hell.

Sadly, though, we seem to have grown grudgingly accustomed to having our mortality catalogued and plotted on charts. The daily broadcast of depressing statistics is encoded with our own impermanence; the infection rates, hospital admissions and heralding of untimely deaths remind us of how precariously life hangs in the balance. Whether that's a good thing or bad thing, I do not know – only that it's been impossible to ignore.

The grinding ubiquity of the pandemic bloated the already distended 24/7 news cycle. The endless unfurling of data, the public health announcements, the fast-moving political battles and the societal friction provided a new baseline for bulletins. Coronavirus gave the media a story that never ended; but, now and then, something appalling would rise above the drone of coverage to remind us that none of us are ever truly safe, plague or no plague.

The loss of five young lives on the last day of school in 2021 in Devonport, Tasmania, was such a moment. A children's jumping castle – hired to make the day at Hillcrest Primary School fun – was blown 10 metres into the air by a freak wind, taking terrified Year Five and Six students with it. That night in Australia, every parent of school-age children hugged their little ones closer and tried not to imagine what the families of the victims were going through.

When I heard the awful news that day, my heart turned not to my own children, by now fully grown, but to Danny and Leila Abdallah and their children. To be honest, they are never far from my thoughts.

When the dust settles, 1 February 2020 will likely be remembered as day one of the 'new normal'. Australians woke that day to the slightly concerning news that the federal government had closed our border to people travelling from China – the first thread of what would become a mesh of rules and restrictions that stopped free movement around the world, around the country and even around our suburbs.

Although the Department of Foreign Affairs and Trade called COVID-19 an 'escalating threat' on that day, the virus remained on the outskirts of conversation. Many saw it as a problem for passengers on far-off cruise ships and people living in Wuhan, and Danny Abdallah paid it little mind. After all, he had enough on his plate.

A busy father of six and a central figure in a sprawling extended family that made their home in Oatlands in Sydney's north-west, Danny was juggling multiple balls as that Saturday dawned hot and humid. He took one of his sons to basketball and one of his daughters to a party. It was also his niece Mabelle's thirteenth birthday, and the kids' cousins were gathering that night for a sleepover at

Danny and Leila's. If that wasn't enough, the adults were due at a twenty-first birthday party for another relative.

As evening approached, the house filled with excited children. Danny and Leila's brood – Antony, thirteen, Angelina, twelve, Liana, ten, Sienna, eight, Alex, five, and Michael, three – were joined by Leila's sister Rania and her husband, Assad Kassas, and three of their four children – birthday girl Mabelle, Charbel, eleven, and Rafqa, four. Filling out the ranks were Danny's cousin Bridget Sakr, her husband, Craig, and her two children, Veronique, eleven, and Michael, thirteen.

'Veronique was our daughter Angelina's best friend,' says Danny. 'They were all close. I can honestly say they're like my own children.'

With a babysitter en route, and the adults trying to prepare for their night out, Danny thought a few moments of quiet might help. 'Leila was getting ready and the kids were making a lot of noise!' he recalls. Danny suggested the children go for a walk to get some ice-cream from a nearby shop. After all, it had been a scorcher, over 40 degrees. 'It was one of the first times I'd actually told them to go for a walk,' Danny says. 'But they were old enough.' Danny put his eldest boy, thirteen-year-old Antony, in charge, handed him some cash and called out, 'Stay together!' as the ice-cream party scurried out the door.

Antony, a gentle soccer-loving boy, shepherded his little sisters and cousins Charbel, Mabelle and Veronique along the footpath of Bettington Road that meandered beneath leafy boughs on the perimeter of Oatlands Golf Club. The littlest Abdallahs, Alex and Michael, were too young for such an adventure. They stayed home with Danny and Leila. Their older cousin Michael Sakr had gone out with his friends.

In a parallel universe just a few blocks away, a local tradesman named Samuel Davidson had spent the day at home. He'd passed the time by his backyard pool, drinking beer and Vodka Cruisers with some mates. It was revealed later that Davidson, twenty-nine, had downed his first alcoholic drink at around 7 am. Many more followed, along with lines of cocaine and MDMA pills throughout the sweltering day. By the time he got behind the wheel of his dual-cab utility that evening, a king tide of booze and drugs was flowing through Davidson's bloodstream, pushing him more than three times over the legal limit to drive.

Shirtless and with a drunken mate along for the ride, Davidson embarked on a chaotic mission to a local service station to withdraw cash. Witnesses said he ran a red light, swerved all over the road, tailgated drivers and sped through the wrong side of a roundabout to overtake a car on Bettington Road. When he lost control and mounted the kerb near the golf club, his two-tonne Mitsubishi Triton was travelling at 133 kph – more than 80 kph above the speed limit. The little cousins never stood a chance.

Back at the Abdallahs' house, Rania was surprised to hear her phone ring just a few minutes after the kids had headed off. It was Mabelle, shrieking hysterically. She said there'd been an accident. Danny grabbed his keys and he and Rania ran to his car and took off down the street. As he turned into Bettington Road he was confronted by an appalling scene in the fading light: the broken bodies of his precious children were strewn along the footpath and a damaged car sat at an awkward angle by the roadside 80 metres away.

The screams of Mabelle and Liana were the only sounds Danny heard. The other kids were motionless and silent. Danny didn't know who to attend to first, and he darted from one crumpled body to the next. Although he knew from the moment he saw each one that they were gone forever, he tried to breathe them back to life all the same.

Another woman, a stranger, was doing CPR on Sienna as Danny performed mouth-to-mouth resuscitation on Antony, his handsome young prince. When the police arrived Danny didn't resist as officers gently moved him aside and covered the four small bodies with tarpaulins;

Antony, Angelina and Sienna Abdallah and their cousin Veronique Sakr had died almost instantly. Charbel and Liana were injured but still breathing while Mabelle was unscathed – physically, at least. Her birthday will likely never be the same as long as she lives.

Before long Leila arrived amid the carnage. Overwhelmed and in shock at what she saw, she could only pray for a miracle: that her children would somehow get up off the ground. As she clambered into the ambulance alongside Liana, Leila convinced herself the others would soon follow.

When she and Liana arrived at Westmead Hospital, Leila waited anxiously for the rest of the kids to be transported. No more ambulances came. After a few minutes she phoned Danny and asked why it was taking so long. He simply told her he'd be there soon. He couldn't bring himself to deliver the devastating truth over the phone.

Minutes later, amid the chaos of the emergency ward, Danny told his wife that their children were dead.

The enormity of what he said was too much for Leila, so she rejected it, refusing to believe her ears. It wasn't until she saw a priest with Danny that reality sunk in. 'She just fell to her knees and screamed. She was hysterical . . .' Danny's voice trails off as the horrific moment replays in his mind. In the time it took Leila to get dressed for a party, three cherished little souls who'd grown inside her, and their adorable cousin, had been snatched away. Liana was going to be okay, but Charbel was now fighting for his life.

As doctors treated Liana, Leila had no doubt Antony, Sienna, Angelina and Veronique were guardian angels watching over her. She knew they were in the operating theatre with Charbel, too. He was in a critical condition with head trauma and surgeons feared he might not survive. It would be two months before he finally woke from a coma with a permanent brain injury.

Danny clearly struggles to find the words to describe their feelings in the aftermath of the tragedy. 'The pain just numbs your whole body, your nerves – everything just disappears,' he says. 'For ten days we didn't eat. Leila actually fainted a few times and ended up in hospital. There is no comparison to it. It's like our heart got amputated out of our bodies.'

I was torn and incredibly wary when I first considered asking the Abdallahs to be part of this book. I worried that inviting them to revisit their dreadful ordeal would cause them more distress. But having watched and listened as they publicly dealt with their suffering and loss with incredible grace, I was convinced they could teach us something profound. After I finally steeled myself to approach them, Danny was as quick as a flash to say yes. 'When we help others we help ourselves,' he told me earnestly.

On a Thursday morning in late 2021, the relaxing of Sydney's COVID restrictions allowed me to visit Danny and Leila at their home. I was nervous as I sat in their kitchen, sipping piping hot Lebanese coffee and surrounded by photos of their departed children. As a journalist you grow accustomed to speaking with people who have endured tragedy, but the Abdallahs' emotional ordeal had been on a scale I'd not encountered before. In the presence of Danny and Leila, I suddenly felt all at sea.

'I think a person's wealth is in their family,' Danny began, smiling warmly, perhaps sensing my discomfort. I smiled back and nodded, willing him to keep talking because I found myself uncharacteristically lost for words.

Danny continued, telling me a bit about himself, and how he runs his own construction company and is responsible for hundreds of employees. He doesn't say this to big-note himself, rather to underscore his point about family. 'I'm a full-time *father*,' he says, holding my gaze with a serious expression, 'and part-time worker.'

Danny and Leila were in the throes of packing when we spoke, just weeks away from moving into a new home. But everywhere I looked there were photos of all six of their children, the last of their treasured possessions to be boxed up.

Although Danny is collected, calm and thoughtful, his Zen-like composure and his commitment to providing for his family belie a far messier youth.

Raised among Housing Commission homes on the hardscrabble streets of Blacktown in Sydney's western suburbs, Danny dropped out of school at the end of Year Ten, opting instead for an apprenticeship as a petty crook. 'I was selling pot at thirteen and stealing cars,' he admits, a little embarrassed and without a hint of bravado. 'By the time I was sixteen my mates were doing stick-ups.'

Although Danny refrained from more serious offences, he willingly immersed himself in gang life. Street fighting was a means of survival and, for the son of Lebanese immigrants, a way of fitting in. 'You're not accepted in the community,' he explains. 'But you're not accepted at home either. You're not connected to your dad because you don't share the same music, you don't watch the same sports.'

Danny sought out other kids who were in the same boat. 'Other people in that world of limbo,' is how he describes them.

His gang was bound by a code of loyalty and vengeance. 'I was aggressive. I was always in fights,' he says, casting his gaze out the window into their tidy backyard. 'That's who I was. I would never take a step back. If some guy hit your mate, you'd go out and get payback.'

Danny somehow managed to stay out of serious trouble and honed his inner warrior by training in martial arts in Australia and Thailand. He shows me photos of a strong, muscled young man in a menacing stance, fists cocked, with a killer stare. Although he used violence on the streets, the discipline of kickboxing and his commitment to the sport also saw Danny win two titles – the East Coast Welterweight title in 1996 and the Australian Welterweight title in 1998.

But at eighteen he got the wake-up call he needed. It came in the form of a violent brawl that shocked him into questioning his future. 'I looked at my brother and some of my extended family and said, "Listen, guys, this isn't for us. This is not how we've been raised. This is not what our parents taught us, these aren't our values."'

Danny found a job in construction, building steel formwork and pouring concrete. But more significantly, he fell under the guidance of the role models he needed. 'I got a really good job with very good people,' he says.

Recognising what a steady hand did for him, Danny is now the first to pass on advice to the men he employs. 'I always say to young kids, "Never choose a job, choose a boss." Young guys need a mentor: someone who will teach them the trade but also someone that's a good father and a good husband.'

Feeling grateful for his job, and the new direction his life was heading in, Danny rekindled his lapsed Catholic faith. 'When you go through some hardship as a kid you tend to become closer to your faith,' he says. 'And that's what brought me closer. I was very grateful from where I was to where I was going. I thank God for it all the time.'

At twenty-six, Danny travelled overseas. His brother Alex was getting married in Cyprus but the pre-wedding celebrations took place in the bride-to-be's hometown in Lebanon. It was at that party – late at night as music filled the room and the dancing crowd surged around him – that Danny spotted a pretty young girl talking with her mother. 'As soon as I saw her I stopped,' he says, grinning broadly at the memory. '*Everything* stopped.'

Leila was nineteen and she'd noticed Danny, too. Although she thought him handsome, she was extremely shy. She didn't speak English and he barely spoke Arabic so it wasn't the most flirtatious first encounter – but something definitely sparked. Danny asked his mother if she knew who the beautiful brunette was. 'Don't even think about it!' she warned him.

'Why did she say that?' I ask.

'Because Mum knew I was a cheeky little boy!' is all Danny will say.

Her main reason, however, was her knowledge that Leila came from a strict family of devout Maronite Catholics, and that she'd even contemplated becoming a nun. Her cheeky little boy couldn't have cared less. Danny felt from the moment he saw her that Leila would be his lifelong partner. The next day he turned up at her family's home and knocked on the door. 'We met,' he says, 'and we just fell in love. I just knew.'

Danny had to fly home two days later, but he was one hundred per cent committed to building a future with Leila. They spoke on the phone every day for the next twelve months. Wary of complications that can come with marrying someone from abroad, Danny's mum asked him why he had to choose his bride from Lebanon. Danny's reply would turn out to be prophetic. 'I said, "Mum, I feel that Leila will stand by me in my darkest hour."'

He returned to Lebanon a year later and the moment he saw Leila again he was certain of their destiny. 'I knew,' he says. 'I knew that this is the girl.' Danny had only four weeks in Lebanon and less than two weeks to arrange the wedding after his proposal. It was a traditional Maronite wedding with 200 guests in attendance.

When Danny flew home, it was without his young bride. It would be another twelve months before her visa was granted. Leila's arrival in Sydney in 2005 was the start of a new chapter in both of their lives. Along with a business partner, Danny started his own construction company and knuckled down to help provide for them. Two months later, Leila was pregnant.

'I remember the first three years Leila was pregnant more than she wasn't,' Danny says. Within nine years the couple were parents to six children. Family was everything to Leila and Danny from the start. He planned his working life around their needs, fastidiously organising his calendar to make himself available on weekends, in school holidays and for sporting events. He even preaches his 'family first' mantra to the young men he employs. 'I tell them, "The biggest decision you make in your life is who you marry."'

Started from the back of a battered two-thousand-dollar ute, Danny's company now does formwork for some of the state's biggest infrastructure projects, a success story he is immensely proud of.

As the business grew, so did his extended family. Five years after Leila immigrated he sponsored her parents to come to Australia, then her brother and his family and, finally, her sister Rania and her family. The men worked together and the families lived just streets apart. 'We'd crank the barbie, get the big speakers and put the music on,' Danny says. 'We'd dance a lot. We were always together and the kids were always playing sport. I was like the grandfather. I was a gatherer with the kids and I'd take them everywhere.'

I laugh and suggest that maybe the title 'uncle' would make him sound younger.

'Yeah!' Danny agrees with a laugh. 'I was a great uncle! I really loved it, you know?'

His devotion to family, religious faith and the affection and respect he has for his beloved Leila have clearly smoothed the sharp edges from the angry young man Danny once was. In the wake of such a senseless tragedy, however, anyone could have forgiven him for defaulting to old settings of rage and revenge. But that's simply not who Danny is anymore, and it's definitely not who Leila ever was.

Just two days after the crash, she returned to the scene of the crime to speak to a nation aghast at her loss. Mountains of bouquets grew on either side of a makeshift shrine on the footpath where the children had died. There was a small table, a statue of Jesus draped in rosary beads, candles, basketballs and framed photographs of four young, sweet faces by the fence of the golf club. As she was physically supported by loved ones, Leila declared her feelings towards the man responsible, Samuel Davidson. 'I don't hate him,' she told the assembled media, her beautiful face pale with grief. 'I think in my heart I forgive him.'

I tell Danny how surprised I was (and, I suspect, millions of Australians were) to hear her speak those words. 'I can honestly say that I don't think I could forgive him, certainly not so soon,' I tell him. 'Nor would I have the strength to face the media and talk about it.'

'Oh, I expected her to say that,' Danny replies quickly. 'Because I know my wife.'

I believe it is the Abdallahs' readiness to forgive and focus on living their best lives that makes their voices so important, particularly in the times we're living through. Their willingness to make peace with the world as best they can in the most dreadful circumstances should serve as a lesson to us all.

Obviously faith plays a huge role. After all, forgiveness lies at the heart of Christianity:

'For if you forgive other people when they sin against you, your heavenly Father will also forgive you' (Matthew 6:14).

But there's much more going on than providence. There's also an element of earthly self-preservation and an innate recognition of the healing powers of forgiveness.

Researchers at Stanford University in the US have studied the effects that offering forgiveness has on people who strive to do it. The Stanford Forgiveness Project shows there is irrefutable evidence that forgiving someone who has hurt you can lead to better physical and mental health. When we forgive we reduce stress, our risk of depression, our anger and even our blood pressure. Conversely, forgiving someone can lead to heightened feelings of compassion, optimism and self-confidence.

Director of the project and author of *Forgive for Good*, Dr Fred Luskin, describes forgiveness as 'an attitude of mind and heart that first feels the suffering of loss, mistreatment or betrayal and then lets it go'. When the suffering is not released, he says, 'It burdens the nervous, cardiovascular and endocrine systems, leading to physical issues over time.'

Of course forgiving someone can be more easily said than done, and it doesn't mean forgetting, nor does it excuse an offence. In Danny and Leila's case, forgiveness went hand in glove with the administration of justice. 'Without justice there's no forgiveness,' says Danny. 'You can't have one without the other.'

The wheels of the judiciary can be slow to turn, and as Danny's family waited for their day in court, they had to find ways to adjust to a world without Antony, Sienna, Angelina and Veronique. Many marriages don't survive the immense emotional upheaval caused by the loss of a child. As Tonya Whitwell pointed out in chapter one, spouses often grieve in vastly different ways, putting more emotional pressure on already strained relationships.

Losing a child goes against the natural order we expect life to follow. The chair of the Sociology Department at Boston University, Deborah Carr, says the death of a child is considered the single worst stressor a person can go through. The anguish of such a loss is deep. A parent is grieving the loss of their child, but also grieving unfulfilled hopes and dreams, potential that will never be realised, experiences that will never be shared. In this case, that suffering was fourfold.

Their faith played a part in keeping them together, but Danny says the affection he and Leila have for their six children also drew them closer together than ever before. They saw and heard in each other glimpses and whispers of those they had lost. 'You look like Antony. You remind me of Angelina. You walk like Sienna. How can I want to be away from you?' Leila once told Danny.

The memory brings a tear to Danny's eye. 'It's just a deep love that we have for each other,' he says softly. 'And that's how we look at each other. I see my daughter Angelina in her. I never want to separate myself from the glimpse of my daughter.'

I ask Danny what else gets him through each day, beyond love and faith. 'Duty and responsibility,' he says without a second's hesitation. He says he needed to stand tall in his role as a father, to keep his 'dad hat' on and make sure everyone else was okay.

Danny knew if he didn't provide the optimism that forgiving Davidson had given him, or if he didn't project the sense of safety children look for in their parents, the toll on the family could have been even higher. 'We had three kids that we lost, but we've still got three kids that we don't want to lose,' he says. 'My wife and I were adamant we would never want our children to say, "The day I lost my siblings, I lost my parents, too."'

That said, it was a heavy burden to carry. Like Curt and Rachel, Danny and Leila alternated in sharing the load, each leaning on the other in their time of need. When Leila was fragile, Danny was strong, and when he was down, she took the baton from him and stood tall for them both. 'I don't know how,' Danny muses, 'but we've never been weak at the same time. We haven't fallen apart together.'

There have been many times when they could have. The nadir came at their children's funerals (just typing those words leaves a lump in my throat). When the service began Danny was inconsolable, choking on tears and literally unable to stand. Leila wrapped her arms around him and whispered in his ear. She reminded him that all they ever wanted to do as parents was get their children to heaven. 'And that's where they are,' she said softly. 'This isn't a funeral, it's a wedding. We need to rejoice. We're going to see them soon.'

The sentiment landed in Danny's heart like sunshine at the height of a storm. 'It made me feel seven feet tall,' he says. He needed to, because worse was yet to come.

Burying children is something no parent should have to face.

'We were at the cemetery and Leila was screaming, my mum was upset, and I remember they were bringing the three coffins to bury them and it was getting a bit out of hand,' Danny recalls. As an undertaker started shovelling dirt onto Antony's coffin amid the wailing of heartbroken relatives, Danny says he heard his eldest son's voice. 'He said, "Dad, I'm not there!"' Danny remembers. 'I went to the undertaker, I took his shovel and I started burying my own children to show everyone. The screaming and crying stopped and you could hear a pin drop. I turned around and said, "Guys, please stop looking down and start looking up. They're in heaven! They're not here."'

Sitting in their kitchen as they recount this moment, I'm amazed at how calm and insightful this beautiful couple is.

I still can't help thinking that if I were in their shoes I'd be twisted with anger at the sheer stupidity of it all. What a terrible price they've paid for some guy's day on the drink. We turn again to the subject of forgiveness.

They both say forgiving Davidson has been key to their survival, individually and as a couple. It was the antidote to the toxic emotions that could easily overcome a vulnerable couple. The Abdallahs say they could ill afford to indulge in hatred. 'I think I had to forgive him for our sake more than his,' says Danny finally. As is his way, Danny also looked at forgiveness through the prism of parental responsibility. 'Raising kids is contagious,' he says. 'They do what you do, not what you say. And I believe if I had an unforgiving heart my kids would catch it and they would end up having an unforgiving heart with each other.'

Although her mum and dad led by example almost immediately after the crash, there was one member of the family who struggled to forgive and accept: the crash survivor, ten-year-old Liana.

'It took her months,' Danny says. Liana was understandably angry and resentful towards Davidson, but Danny and Leila refused to indulge the negative impulses. Slowly but surely, by following the example set by her parents, little Liana eventually understood why she had to let go, too. Danny remembers the day when she informed him she had.

'She said, "Dad, I forgive him, but I don't like him,"' he recalls.

'I said, "That's fine, Liana. That's fine."'

Outwardly Danny didn't want to make a big deal of it, but inwardly he was elated. He'd dreaded the thought that his treasured little girl might be trapped in the past by the bonds of unforgiveness. 'You don't want to shackle your heart with that,' he says, 'because you'll never be able to live and enjoy life to its best potential.'

More than a year after the fateful crash, Samuel Davidson was sentenced to twenty-eight years in prison after pleading guilty to a multitude of charges, including four counts of manslaughter. At his sentencing the judge agreed to read a letter of apology Davidson had written to his victims' families.

While the Abdallahs have forgiven Davidson, it doesn't mean they don't grieve every day, nor does it lessen their loss. I recognise what forgiving the man who killed their children has done for them, but what of Davidson? Has their grace let him off the hook in some way? Have they handed him a moral free pass?

'It's a good question,' says Danny. 'I don't know what it's done to him. I'm not sure how he would feel. I saw him at the court and he looked like a scared little kid. And my daughter said something that day I'll never forget. She said,

"Dad, does he really have to get twenty-eight years?" She felt sorry for him! And as a parent I felt like I'd done my job, because if everyone has that compassion what would the next generation look like?'

I'm in awe of the goodness in the Abdallah family and I ask Danny, only half-jokingly, if he is indeed human.

'I do have flashes of anger even now,' Danny assures me. 'I sometimes get angry with God. "Why would you? Why would this happen to me?" I do ask the whys. That's when I really grieve heavily, and it happens a lot. But then I come out of it and I realise, What's going to change? My kids aren't going to come back.'

'Did vengeance never cross your mind?' I ask. 'Not even once?'

Danny answers by telling me about the night of the accident, after word spread that the driver of the car had been heavily drunk. Riot police were called to Westmead Hospital as an angry mob gathered outside – friends and associates of Danny's who were offering to enact the old gang code of an eye for an eye. It was Danny, not the police, who talked them down. 'I told them the same thing: "It's not going to get my kids back." Besides, there's a saying: "Seek revenge and prepare two graves, including one for yourself." That would only make it worse for my family. That's how I felt at the time and I still feel the same today.'

Danny concedes that this restraint was at odds with his former self, and he likely struggled harder than Leila did in that regard. But in taking the higher road he surprised himself. 'I've learned there are two forms of courage,' he says. 'The first is when you strap on all your armour and you go to battle. But the highest form of courage is when you surrender. When you've got your wife and kids in front of you and you need to make the right decision. I didn't want to lose my whole family. I've lost half. I don't want to lose them all.'

To that end, how does he ever let Alex, Michael and Liana out of his sight nowadays? Danny admits he and Leila are 'a little more protective'; they need to know where their children are at all times. But Danny says he's also a little softer, too. 'I used to give a lot of tough love,' he says. 'You know, "There's a big, bad world out there and I need to get you ready for it!" That's where it's changed. The kids already know it can be a big, bad world.'

As millions of Australians tried to maintain a normal existence through the pandemic, the Abdallahs focused on achieving a deeper, more fundamental goal – they have tried to bring joy back into their lives. After grieving so deeply, Danny says they needed to make a conscious decision to seek happiness. 'You'd think it's the simplest goal but it's probably the most challenging,' he says. 'But we're not going to live a life of sadness and grief. We're entitled to, but we choose not to.'

They go on long family drives. Danny says he turns the music up and sings and tries to make the car shake in time to the beat, anything to make his kids laugh. They play jokes on Leila, play basketball in the driveway, put music on and dance. 'I think we can honestly say we have achieved it,' Danny says, smiling. 'We've got joy back in the household, because that's what our kids would want us to do.'

While the rekindling of joy – alongside forgiveness, faith and justice – has played a major role in Danny and Leila's path to recovery, advocacy has also given them a sense of purpose and direction: the fuel of optimism. They worked with the NSW government in the immediate aftermath of their tragedy to increase the penalties for alcohol- and drug-affected drivers. The 'Four Angels' law was introduced by NSW Parliament one year after the children's deaths. Instead of two separate penalties, the law now compounds drug- and drink-driving charges into one. The fine has been increased, as has the jail term. 'That made me feel very happy,' Danny says. 'I don't think there was a single objection, and it's rare you see that in parliament.'

The Abdallahs have also established a foundation called i4give – the centrepiece being i4give Day, an annual event to encourage others to pursue forgiveness as a pathway to emotional healing. First and foremost it's a day of remembrance for their children, but they also hope it will be an opening for the rest of us to think about a grudge we may be holding and find a way to forgive and set ourselves free.

'I know of brothers and sisters who don't talk to each other, and now their kids, who are cousins, don't talk to each other,' Danny laments. 'It's intergenerational! So we're trying to overcome chronic unforgiveness. It just grabs you and it won't let go, and as long as you don't have a forgiving heart, you'll never reach your greatness as a person.'

So much has changed for the Abdallahs in the last few years, from the profound losses to the more subtle shifts. For one thing, the new house is a lot less cluttered, and it's quieter, too. Both of these facts grate against Danny a little. It goes without saying that the children have experienced immense grief of their own and, before the move, had to adjust to walking past empty bedrooms where their siblings once laughed, played, cried and slept. 'Every single room had a memory,' says Danny.

The family spends as much time as possible at their farm, a tranquil slice of Australian bushland north-west of Sydney where they have built a chapel dedicated to the memory of Antony, Angelina and Sienna.

The biggest change of late, however, is one wrapped up in pure joy. When I first visited the Abdallahs, Leila was five months pregnant. She apologised and excused herself as she wasn't feeling well. With such a precious baby growing inside her, Danny and I of course insisted she go and rest.

'I get emotional thinking about it,' Danny says, his voice starting to break. 'I can't wait.'

All pregnancies are precious, but this one seems to hold so much more significance. Leila had a miscarriage at the end of 2020 – her doctor told her it most likely resulted from all the stress and trauma. Then, in April 2021, the family home was robbed. They really needed some good news to grab on to.

Danny tells me his children are just as excited as he and Leila are. Liana has been shopping for baby clothes, and Alex and Michael couldn't quite manage to keep the secret under wraps. 'We told the boys, "Please don't tell anyone,"' says Danny. 'Anyway, they went to school, they're all praying in religion and Michael puts his hand up and says, "Guys, can we pray for my mum? She's pregnant! But don't tell anyone, it's a secret!"'

Danny throws his head back and roars with laughter. Yes, happiness is most definitely returning, and on 18 March 2022 the Abdallahs welcomed a baby girl, Selina, her name a mix of Sienna and Angelina.

Eight

Kat

When I originally considered producing a book of stories about resilience, love, hope and grace, Kat Barlow was the first person who came to mind. It seems fitting to give her the final word.

Kat blows me away. She is a fun and funny willowy blonde who speaks at a million miles an hour in a lyrical English accent. She only pauses to laugh, and it's clear she has no time to waste. Kat experiences life not only through her own eyes but also through those of her beautiful son, Noah. Most parents have this connection with their child, but Kat's bond with Noah has been fused beyond breaking by the knowledge that her precious boy could be taken from her at any moment.

When he arrived three months early, Noah was beset with so many complex and mysterious health issues that doctors told Kat and her husband, Mark, they didn't know how long he'd survive. Maybe seven months, maybe even seven years, but they all warned the couple that Noah was unlikely to live to see his tenth birthday.

Today their quirky and charming son is twelve and closing in fast on becoming a teenager. Noah's health issues – ranging from brain damage and major food allergies to mitochondrial disease – persist, making it hard for him to walk, eat and process information, but when it comes to finding joy and milking each day for everything it's worth, he's in a class of his own.

I first met the Barlows in 2012 when I interviewed them for *Sunrise*. I was in our Sydney studio, crossing to Kat and Noah at the newsdesk in our Melbourne studio. The story centred on the local community's efforts to rally around the young family and raise funds to help them meet their mounting medical bills.

It was an emotional morning. Kat was so open and honest about their struggles while watching and waiting for Noah to get worse. She described it as being like 'waiting on death row'. During the interview I was increasingly captivated by the cute little boy on Kat's lap with the big glasses and even bigger smile. As Kat talked about their gratitude for the community support, I could tell Noah wasn't at all a fan of the cameras, lights, or having to sit still. He was far more interested in driving his toy truck along the shiny studio desk and trying to wriggle out of Kat's arms, no doubt to find something more interesting to do.

Interviewing the families of sick children is never easy. And as a mother of two – aged eleven and nine when I first spoke to Kat – I always have a moment where I realise 'there but for the grace of God go I'. It could happen to any of us. And illness is so much more heartbreaking when it strikes little ones who haven't even had a chance to live their life or shape their dreams.

The only thing that gives me some comfort is knowing I can help to make a difference – albeit small. I can tell their stories and help raise funds for families or research. I feel useful by lending my profile to charities that support children.

One of them is the Make-A-Wish Foundation, and that's how I came into Noah's world again a few years later. Volunteers from Make-A-Wish had planted a vegetable patch for Noah in the backyard. He was beside himself with delight, revelling in the rich earth, seedlings, sunshine and the perfect place to spend his afternoons. Noah had spent as much time in hospital as he had out since the last time I'd seen him. He was still very fragile but, despite gloomy prognoses, he'd bloomed into a lovely boy. The wriggly truck driver of years past was now a keen and thoughtful gardener.

When I contacted Kat again in 2020 to ask if she'd be willing to share their journey together in a book, I explained that I hoped her experiences and wisdom would benefit others who find themselves facing uphill battles in life. Kat agreed in a heartbeat, but told me the life lessons she had to share weren't really hers, they were Noah's.

On the day we start our interviews, Kat shows me a photo of Noah as a fierce Viking. He's standing on the coffee table, his frail body extended to its full height, emboldened by his inner warrior. His arms are thrust skywards in victory, a plastic sword aloft in one hand, a cardboard shield in the other. The triumphant pose is exactly as he'd envisaged it when he started planning his day. Noah even went to the trouble of drawing a sketch so Kat, his props designer, knew how he wanted the moment to look.

The New South Wales–Victoria border is closed due to COVID so we've been forced to speak over Zoom (I'd like to thank its creators, by the way, for keeping people connected). In a video she shows me, Kat encourages Viking Noah to shout louder as she uses her phone to film his conquest of the lounge room. It dawns on me they are making memories, and Kat is souveniring another moment from another cherished day.

For this family, every rotation of the planet is a monumental blessing; every day is a bonus that needs to be celebrated and mined for every last skerrick of togetherness. As Noah likes to say, 'Let's just do today, shall we? Let's start there.'

Clearly, Noah is one of a kind, but I don't think I've ever met anyone like Kat either. She looks for the silver lining in *every* cloud, no matter how ominous. She has come to realise there is joy to be harvested even in the most barren places. It's something Noah seems to have always known.

Noah still has difficulty walking, thinking, breathing and eating. He's fed through a tube that leads directly into his stomach, and he requires a hoist to get out of bed and vision domes to read. But Kat refuses to see these as 'special needs' and instead refers to Noah's range of therapies as 'upgrades' that only serve to make him more extraordinary.

She also refuses to dwell on what could have been, what should have been, or wonder why fate cast a shadow of death over her little family. Those are things she can't control, so Kat channels all of her energy into 'celebrating what is'. By doing this she says she has found a way to re-imagine the hand her family has been dealt and find a measure of peace and happiness.

'You make it sound like everyone could face these things the way you do, when I'm not sure that I could,' I tell her.

Kat smiles at me over the internet and tries to explain. 'I positively reinterpret something that's happened with optimism and acceptance, and look for coping mechanisms,' she says. 'I focus on the problem head-on rather than ignoring it, or hiding from it, and saying, "This is not fair!" or "This is awful!"'

In other words, she takes the good and leaves the bad, but I'm still unsure how she manages when there has been so much bad for so long. Kat points to Noah's history of strokes as an example. He's had eight stroke-like episodes since the age of two, and, after each one, he had to learn to walk again. As Kat talks me through this I can't even begin to imagine what it would be like to go through that as a mother just once. Kat has a remarkable take, though: 'I've had the honour of watching him learn to walk – *eight times!*' she marvels. 'Usually children learn to walk and that's it, you get excited that one day and then it's done. Well, I've had the privilege of looking at him constantly and going, "Far out, he's such a bad-arse! Look at him walk today!"'

When I remark that this is possibly the greatest example of staying positive I have ever heard, Kat gently corrects me. Her outlook isn't so much positive as it is optimistic. 'Optimism is a mindset that helps you reinterpret what is happening,' she says. 'Optimism is to look for what else is true and settle upon something different for your soul.'

While it's true none of us know what tomorrow may bring, or how many breaths we have left to take, time doesn't hang over most people the way it does the Barlows. Kat calls this 'living grief'.

'It's all the things that grief is, but it never ends,' she says. 'It's denial, it's anger and deep sadness, but you have to find a way to live with it, every day.'

'Where on earth did you even begin?' I ask.

Like so many others in this book, Kat says the first step was acceptance. 'Wishing things were different, wishing things were better, wishing things were easier will always lead to pain and suffering,' she says adamantly. 'You can argue with reality but you're going to be wrong one hundred per cent of the time. It is what it is.'

Once she accepted reality and gravely absorbed the prognosis that Noah was unlikely to see ten, Kat decided the next step had to be a complete recalibration of her outlook. 'We had to focus on what we *have*, not on what we "lost",' she says, wiggling her fingers to make quotation marks.

'We had to cherish the gift that we have, not the gift that we expected.'

It's a shift in thinking Kat calls 'the Elsa method', referencing *Frozen*, once one of Noah's favourite films (but not so much now that he's grown up, he tells me). 'It's literally "Let it go!"' she says in a sing-song voice and with a little laugh. 'We used to sing it when there was darkness or pain and we needed to move through it after feeling the sads.' Yet while she says there's nothing to be gained from dwelling on how things might have been, the reality is still very painful. 'Sometimes it will break you and that day you will sob and be on your knees, and you will beg for it to stop,' she admits. 'But we cannot change what is true.'

All the Barlows can do is face each day as it comes, which is why Noah is standing on a table dressed as a Viking. Instead of a bucket list – a term that has an unhelpful sense of finality about it – Noah has a 'living list': a carefully curated agenda of all the things he dearly wants to do. Today his great desire is to be an ancient Scandinavian warrior, but Noah has many more dreams to fulfil. He has already hugged a seal, and plans to drive a dump truck, then go fishing . . . fabulous ambitions for a growing boy and priceless memories for Kat and Mark.

Kat reckons everyone, regardless of what stage of life they're in, should follow Noah's lead and draw up a living list. 'We ought to do more of it!' she implores. 'Stop in those moments and say, "Let's do something really silly. Now!" You miss so much by thinking we have time. None of us really have time.'

To help keep the momentum up the Barlows have also instituted 'Never Say No Fridays', when Kat and Mark agree to do whatever Noah's heart desires. They've spent hours fulfilling wishes like walking up and down the aisles at Bunnings, examining every nut, bolt and tool on display. They've spent long afternoons just sitting on the grass in the park watching other kids, and they've savoured plenty of Fridays at home happily playing spaceships. Simple, peaceful and memorable.

Catherine Nagle was born and raised in Manchester in the cold north-west of England. At twenty-six she came to Australia for a holiday. After landing in Perth on a 42-degree day, she decided Melbourne might be a better fit for her. At Spencer Street station she jumped on a tram to St Kilda Beach and rode it to the end of the line. When it stopped near the sands of Port Phillip Bay, Kat decided that was where she would live. 'I call it "following your bliss",' she says with a chuckle.

Kat quickly fell in love with the country, and then a ute-driving Aussie named Mark Barlow. In the early days of dating, he made her a sculpture that almost miraculously resembled a mythical creature she used to draw as a child. Mark called his creation a 'Mugwump', and so had Kat. It turned out the couple had spent their childhood drawing exactly the same thing on opposite sides of the planet. 'The shapes were the same, the stories were similar, everything!' Kat exclaims. 'We just thought, "What is happening?"'

Needless to say, they called each other Mugwump. 'That's how we came together, and we created another Mugwump with Noah,' Kat says.

Three years after they wed, Noah arrived following a gruelling IVF process. Kat looks back on the testing experience with her trademark optimism. 'I got to see him be implanted, to go into my womb, which is extraordinary!' she beams.

Like many people, Kat and Mark talked about all the possibilities before they decided to become parents. They wanted a little person so badly they tried to be open to every possibility, including the possibility of having a child with additional needs.

Nothing, however, could have readied them for the crisis that unfolded during Kat's pregnancy. She developed pre-eclampsia, dangerously high blood pressure that very quickly developed into eclampsia, a life-threatening condition. Her baby stopped growing and at twenty-nine weeks Kat underwent an emergency caesarean. 'Talk about blazing into the world in an extraordinary fashion!' Kat says with a smile and a theatrical roll of her eyes.

Her dangerously premature little boy was rushed away before Kat could even lay eyes on him. For days all she had was a photo of Noah, taken in the Neonatal Intensive Care Unit at The Royal Women's Hospital, where a web of tubes connected him to machines that kept him alive. 'I just kept thinking, "How will I know he's mine? I don't even know what he looks like! I haven't met him and he's out there!"' Kat recalls. 'But, of course, you know as soon as you see them.'

Noah was delivered weighing just 1090 grams, and by the time Kat finally met him three days later his weight had fallen to 860 grams. The memory is a hard one for Kat. After a big intake of air she tells me, '*That* was the start of our extraordinary adventure into the unknown.'

It was two months before Kat and Mark could take Noah home, but he wasn't there for long. They were constantly in and out of hospital over the following years as doctors tried to come to grips with his complex and baffling conditions. Noah had problems feeding and appeared, alarmingly, to be allergic to all food. They were still in hospital on his first birthday when his feeding tube was inserted, and for years he was fed a special formula of amino acids and vitamins.

Not long after his second birthday, Noah had his first stroke-like episode. He'd been sitting in his pram laughing when Kat noticed only one side of his face was lit up with his beautiful smile. She plucked him out of the pram and tried to stand him up, but Noah's left leg wouldn't move. Doctors later described it as a mini stroke, and Kat and Mark insisted on an MRI scan. Ten days later, Kat was at home alone with Noah when the doctor called with some devastating news. The scan revealed Noah had suffered catastrophic damage to his brainstem – the part of the brain that doesn't rejuvenate. There was concern over how much longer he would live.

Initially Kat and Mark fell apart emotionally. Kat remembers being absolutely broken for two weeks solid – time they spent looking at their precious baby boy, sobbing and questioning their own strength. 'I remember saying, "I don't know how to do this. I cannot do this. I don't know how to love him through this,"' Kat admits.

After a while, though, Kat and Mark slowly picked themselves up off the floor, knowing they couldn't continue like that. The only way to honour their son, they resolved, was to throw themselves into the life they had always wanted to have with him. That was the moment of acceptance, followed by a recalibration of their thinking. 'The truth is Noah's condition was a terrible gift,' says Kat. 'It's the gift you would never wish on another human being, and that's why it's terrible. But it's also a gift, because we look at things differently to other people. We choose to live life intentionally. We choose to make memories every day.'

Every stage of Noah's development has brought new struggles. When he attempted to walk at eighteen months old, his muscles would spasm and he'd collapse on the floor. Meanwhile persistent complications with his feeding and nutrition meant he was constantly being hospitalised. Finally, at the age of seven, Noah was diagnosed with mitochondrial disease, complex I.

There are thousands of mitochondria in nearly every cell in our bodies and they produce 90 per cent of the energy we need to function. When mitochondria don't work properly, cells begin to die until, eventually, entire organ systems fail. Mitochondrial disease is a debilitating condition that varies in its severity. Complex I – the disease Noah is suffering – typically affects the nervous system, the heart and skeletal muscles. There is no cure.

Noah's condition is deteriorating, sometimes quite dramatically. Each metabolic stroke causes more brain damage, and the simple process of growing older and bigger takes a lot out of him. 'It can be little things that you don't really notice, and then other things are confronting,' says Kat. 'Like the sight in his left eye just went one day. Gone!

And he got another spinal lesion, which meant he couldn't walk anymore, so then he needed surgery. That happened in twenty-four hours, from being able to move to then not.'

There are still so many unknowns about Noah's condition, but nowadays when doctors offer a new prognosis, Kat and Mark politely decline the information. The Barlows see no benefit in knowing when the end will come for Noah. They prefer the optimism that arrives with the sun each day.

'What if I'd spent the last year of COVID lockdowns going, "We've missed all this stuff and this could have been his last year?"' says Kat. 'While it is hard, it wouldn't have helped our mental health to do that. You know, "They're not doing the school concert! This might have been his last one! We couldn't do Easter? Might have been our last one together! Can't be around people for Christmas? Might have been our last one!" So I declined the prognosis because Noah will walk his own path, and it may be tomorrow, and it might be a year, but it's his to walk without conditions or a clock attached.'

Raising a child who has extra needs is profoundly challenging. It's estimated just over 7 per cent of Australia's children have a disability or developmental delay. Caring for them can be isolating, gruelling, nerve-racking and constant, and Kat tells me she had a lot to learn. She refuses, however, to say it's hard. 'It's only hard for Noah,' she says. 'For me it's simply a logistical challenge.'

Kat likens it to being thrown into a job you know nothing about. 'It's a case of, "Tomorrow you're going to be a quantum physicist. You start at the rocket ship tomorrow morning and if the rocket crashes, everyone's going to die and it's on you!"' she says, laughing. 'You have to learn the required skills – and quickly!'

Kat's day usually starts with a hungry boy calling out from his bedroom. 'I have to go and unplug his tube and get him out of bed and then decide if he needs a walker or a wheelchair or if he needs a hoist and where we're at today because mitochondrial disease is a changeable thing.'

Noah's breakfast is a blend of nutrition, medication and vitamins, fed directly into his stomach. When breakfast is out of the way, Kat focuses on whether he's well enough to go to school that day and, if she gives him the thumbs up, the morning starts to look a little more like that of any other schoolkid: there's the frenzy to locate the hat, find socks and shoes and pack a lunch box, although Kat *does* have the extra step of medical equipment on the checklist.

'I'm also asking, "Where's your icebag? Where's your ice vest? Where's your wheelchair? Have you got both your wheelchairs? Where are your AFOs? Have you got your other computer? Have you got your dome magnifier to be able to see? Have you got both pairs of glasses with you? Where is your emergency kit? Have you got your tube on? Have you got all of *that* stuff?"'

Kat makes me laugh, and also feel a little embarrassed, as she rattles off the list of needs. I can't tell you how many times I lost my cool when my kids couldn't find their library books or their lunch box, or I discovered a half-eaten-and-now-mouldy sandwich in their schoolbag. It's easy to write off those mundane everyday tasks as annoying, even infuriating. But not for Kat: in her world the ordinary is a joy. Where I might get miffed when someone puts an empty container back in the fridge, Kat says she cries with happiness if Noah asks her for a snack. You understand why when she explains that he didn't eat any food until he was seven, when, finally, she found one that was safe for him to have.

Indeed it was only a week before we started our interviews that Noah ate his lunch at school for the first time. Kat had packed a lunch box for him since kindergarten – fully aware he couldn't eat it – simply because she knew he didn't want to be different from the other kids. Sometimes he'd move the food around a bit, while on other days it came home with him completely untouched. No wonder the first-ever school lunch was cause for celebration. 'That's another example of living grief,' Kat points out. 'It's the honour and the privilege of noticing the small things because they're not small, they're bloody *huge*.'

I realise school means the world to Noah but, in an echo of the Abdallahs' profound losses, I wonder how Kat manages to let her darling boy out of her sight between the hours of 9 am and 3 pm. 'Do you have to fight the urge to wrap him up and keep him close?' I ask.

'Borrowed time is what I call him being at school,' she replies. 'I could choose to be that parent and not let him go – I *do* want him with me. I *want* to look at him, I *want* to touch him, I want to just have every moment of my soul and self with him. Yeah, I could choose that, but who would that be for? Not for him. That would be totally selfish and all about me.'

Kat recognises Noah needs friends as much as any child, maybe even more so. He needs to play games and cram as much into his days as he can. 'That stuff is his "ordinary",' Kat says. 'His friends are everything to him, and having those moments with them is more important than anything that I could come up with at home.'

When Noah was four and particularly unwell, he insisted on going to kindergarten whenever he wasn't in hospital. 'He would go to kindy a few days at a time and I would sit with him and be so thankful for the people sharing this journey with us,' she says.

As strong and optimistic as Kat is, she breaks down when she tells me about the impact Noah has on those around him. Through tears of pride, or perhaps even awe, she says he moves everyone he meets 'deeply and forever, because of the way he shows up for other people'. In February 2022, Noah was voted school captain. 'He knows he brings smiles to everyone,' says Kat. 'Imagine if I'd just kept him all for myself? What a dishonourable way to be.'

Although it's a constant, living grief can surprise, too, and there are moments that hit Kat like a bolt of lightning; reality checks that fall out of the clear blue sky. 'It could be a stranger in a supermarket asking Noah how old he is,' she says. 'It takes my breath away, because doctors said he'd never make it to ten. Ever!'

At times like that Kat is transported back to her gravely ill son's hospital bedside as doctors told her it was time to say goodbye to him. 'We have lived that moment,' she says softly. 'More than once.'

There have been moments at the shops when people have asked Noah what he wants to be when he grows up. As much as he loves Vikings, he's had his heart set on joining the Australian Army. Kat recalls him holding forth on his future military career to an inquisitive stranger, as he sat in his wheelchair with its plastic leg supports. Afterwards the woman said, 'Cool! You're going to be an officer, or a medic?' But Noah was adamant he'd be a soldier on the ground, running around.

'Those are the moments of living grief,' says Kat. 'It's like a whisper of a moment because in my head I imagine "What if?" or think, "It shouldn't be like this – he *should* be able to choose that path." And then you have to stop and remind yourself, "He's many things, all beautiful things. Let's focus on all the wonderful things that he is and that he *can* do."'

Fortunately, life has a way of smoothing out some of the sharp edges. Two days after that encounter with the stranger at the supermarket, Noah told Kat he'd shelved his plans for a life in the army. 'I said, "Okay. Why?" And he said, "I hate cargo nets and I don't want to be flung upside down." And that was it! We forget that they're kids and change their minds probably more often than their pants.'

Sometimes, however, situations and conversations arise that take Kat close to her breaking point. She and Mark have never discussed the 'alternate future' with their son – the one the doctors have long warned them is imminent. 'We've never walked that with him,' Kat says with a firm shake of her head. 'We've never let him believe that he can't, or that life is anything other than extraordinary and anything you want it to be. We just don't.'

Recently Noah casually asked her how old he'd be in 2050. Kat had to walk away and take a moment for herself. 'Sometimes it floors you and you have to take a breath and say, "I just need to go to the toilet for a second,"' she says. 'And then you just sit and breathe and go, "Oooh, okay. It is what it is. It is what it is. It is what it is." And then you come out, tell him he'll be forty in the year 2050, and you carry on with your life again.'

I have to wipe away a tear at this point but, extraordinarily, Kat assures me that gut-wrenching moments like that are a glorious gift. 'Part of the privilege of having a child like Noah is you *get* to feel that way,' she says. 'And part of the privilege is I get to be broken by those moments, I get to have those moments.'

'I don't know how you do it,' I say.

'When I need to have a cry, I will stand in the shower and I will sob and I will literally make time to have those moments,' Kat explains. 'There have been times I've said to Noah, "Today I can't do this. I don't know how to do this, I just need space." And we'll sit and I'll cry.'

It's important, she says, not to hide our feelings from our children. 'How can you teach them resilience when you don't show them what pain looks like, and then how you walk your steps through it?' she asks. 'I will cry and say, "Mummy's just really sad today because this happened or that happened, and it's really challenging." And he'll ask, "Well, what do we do?" And I say, "We don't do anything. We just sit in the pain for a minute and we reflect on what is and then we walk the steps out of that into another moment.""

True resilience, Kat says, 'lives in the experience of feeling those emotions and not numbing them'. The key to coping lies in regulating those feelings. While some days can appear overwhelming, Kat has learned to take herself to a safe place where the emotional temperature is not too hot, not too cold. 'It's what I call my middle ground,' she says. 'It's not happy and it's not sad. I just need the middle space.'

And when she finds it, Kat looks for ways to climb higher. 'It's singing at the top of my voice, or putting on nineties hip-hop music and shaking my arse, or going for a walk with our dog, Larry Pancakes,' she says. 'I also watch a lot of stand-up comedy. To not feel is to be numb. There's suffering, absolutely, and there's pain. But there's definitely a choice in what's next. Always.'

Although they know the worst pain lies ahead of them, Kat and Mark don't ever dwell on the fact their brave and delightful son will someday leave them. Kat keeps a list of all the funny things Noah says. She videos him on the fifteenth of every month and has edited a decade of clips into a two-minute montage of his growth since he was born. She scans his drawings, but keeps his favourite one with her always. It's tattooed on the inside of her left wrist, closest to her heart.

'Noah says it's him naked in the street, but he's got pants on and a scarf in case he gets cold,' Kat explains as she holds her wrist up to her laptop for me to see. 'He'll always tell people, "Mummy has a tattoo of me naked on her arm!" He tells everyone, because he knows it's funny.'

While Kat focuses on every blessed day with Noah, she realises her total immersion in his life is likely to leave her stranded in some ways when he's gone. 'How can I survive this afterwards?' she ponders out loud. 'What will my life look like? At the moment my whole soul, my whole world, is only him. Other people have different things going on as well: maybe it's a hobby, other kids, a job, a career. I don't, because what is happening is so intense that I don't ever think of anything else outside of him.'

Even so, Kat knows she and Mark are not alone, and in 2018 she founded Empowerment Ethos – an online hub that helps other parents of disabled, sick or terminally ill children find peace, direction and happiness on their respective journeys. Kat shares her own experiences, runs a support group forum as a safe place to vent, and offers self-empowerment courses that help people explore their own mindset and coping mechanisms.

'I used to get asked a lot, "How do you stay positive?"' says Kat. 'And I thought, "Well, I don't, but let me think about it."' Realising there was a dearth of online support for parents and carers, she trained in human development and life coaching, and started telling their story. Empowerment Ethos, she says, will be Noah's legacy. 'It's how his voice, his lessons and his message will live on beyond either of us.'

It's also likely to give Kat some purpose and direction when he's gone. 'What will I do to survive?' she asks. 'Because I don't know how I'll make it. How can you make it? How can you possibly survive that when he's my only child? And he's all there will ever be? How do you create something outside of yourself?'

There is no answer now, of course. Only time will tell.

For all that she's been through and all that lies ahead, Kat believes it was her calling to be Noah's mum, and to pass on to others what he has taught her about bravery, resilience, acceptance and love. 'I think it was always meant to be,' she says reflectively. 'I don't think the universe makes mistakes. I think that you are gifted the life experience to walk it for your own lessons, or to teach other people, and everybody's survival story is somebody else's guide.'

'With Noah's birth I signed an unwritten contract with him that I will carry the burden of his death by loving him in the way that he deserves, because that's what love is. If you have a relationship with anybody that you will walk with – your children or your spouse – you will love them with your whole soul and your whole self, even if it's too much, and you don't hold back.'

Love is also about finding a way through the hardest of times. A few years back, overwhelmed by their circumstances, Kat and Mark gradually disconnected from one another. Mark was working hard and travelling a lot while Kat was home full-time with Noah. The distance created a gap and the stress became a wedge that pushed them to a place where many couples with complex children find themselves.

It's reported that having a child with additional needs can increase a couple's chance of divorce, but only slightly, according to an article in the *American Journal on Intellectual and Developmental Disabilities*. While the COVID lockdowns and border closures of 2020 were a curse to millions of Australians, they proved a blessing to the Barlows. Restrictions put an end to Mark's travel, and lockdowns brought them precious time together. Today Kat and Mark are stronger than ever and have their arms wrapped around their most precious creation.

It's not surprising that when Kat is struggling she asks herself a simple question: What would love do?

'If I feel exhausted, if I feel so tired I can't move, if I can't function: "What would love do?"' she says. 'Love would take a bath. Love would take a deep breath, love would have a cry then put on a movie that I know is going to make me laugh. That is love for myself in those moments. That is self-compassion.'

It's one of the things she teaches at Empowerment Ethos. 'We need to ask ourselves, "What would I say or how would I care for my best friend?"' says Kat. 'Self-compassion is doing that for ourselves.'

Or, if we can't quite manage that, Kat says we could start small, the way Noah does when he's feeling up against it. Despite a lifetime of hospital visits he still hates blood tests. On the way to his last appointment Kat asked him how he was planning to summon the courage to face another needle.

'He said, "I just need to find my fifteen seconds of brave, Mum,"' Kat recalls.

When she asked what he meant, Noah explained how he toughed out challenges like a needle in the arm by counting to fifteen, by which time it would usually be over.

'But what if it takes longer?' she asked him.

'Then I'll choose to be brave again,' he said. 'But after a minute, I'm done!'

Fifteen seconds of brave. I reckon we can all try that.

Resources

Adult

Lifeline
13 11 14
lifeline.org.au

Suicide Call Back Service
1300 659 467
suicidecallbackservice.org.au

Beyond Blue

1300 22 4636

beyondblue.org.au

MensLine Australia

1300 78 99 78

mensline.org.au

1800RESPECT

1800 737 732

1800respect.org.au

Youth

Kids Helpline

1800 551 800

kidshelpline.com.au

headspace

1800 650 890

headspace.org.au

ReachOut

au.reachout.com

Other resources

Life in Mind (suicide prevention portal)
lifeinmindaustralia.com.au

Head to Health (mental health portal)
headtohealth.gov.au

SANE (online forums)
sane.org

Acknowledgements

To Tonya, Grace, Juli, Aurelio, Rachel, Chloe, Danny and Kat, I hope you know how incredible you all are, how strong, positive and wise. Thank you for trusting me with your stories, but most importantly thank you for sharing them with us all. I know it wasn't always easy, but I have no doubt your words will bring comfort to so many who need a little courage and inspiration. Thank you for being brave when you needed to be for you, and again when we needed you to be for us.

It's taken a while for this book to come to life. Some of these stories I have held close to my heart and have been waiting to write for many years. Thank you, Penguin, for believing in such a precious project and giving me the time necessary to ensure everyone was comfortable going back through some pretty traumatic experiences. There have been many tears – plenty during the interviews, as we stepped into those dark places, but just as many as we celebrated the sunshine at the end.

Sophie Ambrose – you understood what I wanted to write from the very first moment we met. Thank you for loving each person in this book as I have. Craig Henderson – thank you for making these stories shine while keeping heart at the very centre of every word. You are a gifted wordsmith and it was an honour to work with you. Melissa Lane – thank you for bringing it all together; and Christa Moffitt – thank you for the beautiful cover art.

My managers, James Erskine and Martin Criss – I appreciate your guidance and support always, thank you.

World Vision, who introduced me to Grace, and Make-A-Wish, who introduced me to Kat – I am beyond proud to be your ambassador.

But most of all, thank you to my family. My husband, John, and my children, Nick and Talia – you make me brave every single day. I love you.

Melissa Doyle is an award-winning journalist with more than thirty years' experience. She is one of the most well-known and trusted people in the Australian media. As co-host of Channel 7's *Sunrise* she covered such significant events as the Beaconsfield mine disaster, the wedding of Prince William and Catherine Middleton, four Olympic Games, the Queen's Diamond Jubilee, the Queensland floods, Victoria's Black Saturday bushfires, multiple federal and state elections, the inauguration of Barack Obama and the election of Pope Francis.

Melissa joined the Seven Network's news team in 2013. She and the team were recognised with a Walkley Award, a Logie and three international Edward R. Murrow Awards for their live rolling coverage of the Lindt Café siege.

In more recent years Melissa has been a host and senior correspondent for the Seven Network's flagship news and public affairs program *Sunday Night*, and narrated Channel 9's *Australia Behind Bars*. She is currently filming *This Is Your Life* for Channel 7 and is the weekend breakfast host for radio station smoothfm.

Discover a
new favourite

Visit **penguin.com.au/readmore**